ADVANCED

lighthouse 3

Grammarmaster

Deinen Grammarmaster findest du auch in der **Cornelsen Lernen App**.

Siehst du eines dieser Symbole in deinem Grammarmaster, findest du in der App …

   alle **Erklärfilme**

   Lösungen zu den Aufgaben

Cornelsen

ADVANCED
lighthouse 3

Grammarmaster

Im Auftrag des Verlages erarbeitet von
James Styring, Charlbury

In Zusammenarbeit mit der Englischredaktion
Klaus Unger (Projektleitung), Anja Zieschang

Beratende Mitwirkung
Daniel Henn, Frankfurt/Main; Christina Sieber, Schorndorf

Lizenzmanagement
Silke Kirchhoff

Illustrationen
Matthias Pflügner, Berlin
Irina Zinner, Hamburg

Fotos
Chocolate Films, London

Umschlaggestaltung
Rosendahl, Berlin

Layoutkonzept
Klein & Halm, Berlin

Layout und technische Umsetzung
Compuscript Ireland and Chennai

Druck
Drukarnia Dimograf Sp. z o.o., Bielsko-Biała

PEFC-zertifiziert
Dieses Produkt stammt aus nachhaltig bewirtschafteten Wäldern und kontrollierten Quellen
PEFC/32-31-076
www.pefc.pl

www.cornelsen.de

Soweit in diesem Lehrwerk Personen fotografisch abgebildet sind und ihnen von der Redaktion fiktive Namen, Berufe, Dialoge und Ähnliches zugeordnet oder diese Personen in bestimmte Kontexte gesetzt werden, dienen diese Zuordnungen und Darstellungen ausschließlich der Veranschaulichung und dem besseren Verständnis des Buchinhaltes.

Dieses Werk berücksichtigt die Regeln der reformierten Rechtschreibung und Zeichensetzung.

Die Webseiten Dritter, deren Internetadressen in diesem Lehrwerk angegeben sind, wurden vor Drucklegung sorgfältig geprüft. Der Verlag übernimmt keine Gewähr für die Aktualität und den Inhalt dieser Seiten oder solcher, die mit ihnen verlinkt sind.

Alle Drucke dieser Auflage sind inhaltlich unverändert und können im Unterricht nebeneinander verwendet werden.

© 2024 Cornelsen Verlag GmbH, Mecklenburgische Str. 53, 14197 Berlin, E-Mail: service@cornelsen.de

1. Auflage, 2. Druck 2024
978-3-06-034609-7

Unit 1
London: City life

Unit 2
Manchester: Who we are

Unit 3
Scotland: Adventure

Unit 4
Wales: Digital life

Unit 5
Two Irelands: Together

Auf einen Blick

Erklär-film

REVISION: Die Zukunft mit *will* (The will-future)

Das *will-future* verwendest du für Dinge, die vermutlich in der Zukunft geschehen werden, oder für spontane Entschlüsse und Hilfsangebote. Du bildest es mit *will* und dem Infinitiv des Verbs.

A **Bejahte Aussagesätze** *(Positive statements)*			B **Verneinte Aussagesätze** *(Negative statements)*		
We	will / 'll	go hiking.	We	will not / won't	go hiking.
It	will / 'll	be sunny tomorrow.	It	will not / won't	be sunny tomorrow.

► SB p. 17, p. 43, p. 186

---

1 REVISION **Pearl's journey from Covent Garden to Camden Market**

Complete the description with positive or negative forms of the will-future.

Pearl (1) *will meet*_____ (meet) her friends at about 3.30 on Saturday

afternoon. She (2) _____ (not take) a taxi from Covent Garden to

Camden Market and she (3) _____ (not go) by bus.

Instead, she (4) _____ (walk) from Covent Garden to Leicester Square tube station.

There she (5) _____ (catch) the Northern Line tube towards Camden.

Pearl

---

2 REVISION **Decisions, offers and other situations**

Write sentences. Use the positive or negative forms of the *will*-future.

1 **Khalif**: It's raining. I don't want to play football in the rain!

   Dexter: It's OK. *we / not play / football today* <u>We won't play football today.</u>

2 **Caleb**: I can't find my phone.

   Elliot: *I / help / you to find it* _____

3 **Kayden**: This test is difficult.

   Ahmed: Yes, it is. *I / not get / more than 75 %* _____

4 **Poppy**: What's the weather like?

   Isabel: *I think it / be / sunny later* _____

► Check

REVISION: Die Zukunft mit *will*: Fragen und Kurzantworten *(Questions and short answers)*

Bei Fragen stellt du *will* an den Satzanfang. Hat die Frage ein Fragewort, steht dieses noch vor *will*.

Will they *go* shopping? – Yes, they *will*. / No, they *won't*.
Will she *visit* her grandmother? – Yes, she *will*. / No, she *won't*.
Who will you invite to your party?
When will we arrive in London?

▶ SB p. 17, p. 43, p. 186

3 REVISION **A trip to London**

The three students are in London this week. Look at the chart. What will they do?

a) Write questions with the *will*-future.

b) Write short answers.

	Omar Yes	Omar No	Dylan Yes	Dylan No	Grace Yes	Grace No
visit Big Ben	✓			✕	✓	
go on the Orbit Slide	✓		✓			✕
look at the graffiti in the Leake Street Tunnel	✓		✓			✕
go to the South Bank	✓		✓		✓	
have a ride on the London Eye		✕	✓		✓	
visit the Houses of Parliament	✓			✕		✕

1 Omar / Big Ben?

   Will Omar visit Big Ben? _____ *Yes, he will.* _____ .

2 Grace / Orbit Slide?

   _____ _____ .

3 Dylan and Omar / Leake Street Tunnel?

   _____ _____ .

4 Grace and Omar / South Bank?

   _____ _____ .

5 Omar / London Eye?

   _____ _____ .

6 Grace and Dylan / Houses of Parliament?

   _____ _____ .

▶ Check ↻

Bedingungssätze Typ I *(Conditional sentences type I)*

Mit Bedingungssätzen sagst du, was unter bestimmten Bedingungen geschehen wird: *Falls ... dann.*

Bedingungssätze bestehen aus zwei Teilen:
- einem Nebensatz mit *if (if-clause)* im *simple present*, der die Bedingung nennt,
- einem Hauptsatz *(main clause)* mit *will*, *'ll* oder *won't*, der die Folge nennt.

Der Nebensatz *(if-clause)* kann auch <u>nach</u> dem Hauptsatz *(main clause)* stehen. Dann setzt du kein Komma.

Bedingung *(if-clause)* → Folge *(main clause)*	Folge *(main clause)* ← Bedingung *(if-clause)*
If you need help, I'll be there.	*I'll be there if you need help.*
(Falls du Hilfe brauchst, bin ich da.)	*(Ich bin da, falls du Hilfe brauchst.)*
If the bus is too late, we'll miss the train.	*We'll miss the train if the bus is too late.*
(Falls der Bus zu spät ist, verpassen wir den Zug.)	*(Wir verpassen den Zug, falls der Bus zu spät ist.)*

► SB p. 21, p. 187

4 Advice for visitors to London

a) (Circle) the right conditional forms.

1 If you go to Trafalgar Square, you ('ll see)/ see Nelson's Column.

2 You go / 'll go past the London Eye if you walk along the South Bank.

3 If you don't join / join the Ghost Bus tour, you'll miss all the scary stories!

4 If you buy your tube ticket with a credit card, you save / 'll save money.

Trafalgar Square

5 You'll be able to use public transport all day if you have / will have a Travelcard.

6 If you don't have / won't have any money, you'll be able to get into most museums – lots of them are free.

b) **Complete the sentences. Use the simple present or will-future form of the verbs.**

1 If you go by bus, you *'ll get* _____ (get) a good view of London from the top of

a double-decker.

2 You'll see some famous black birds called 'ravens' if you _____ (visit)

the Tower of London.

3 If you _____ (like) skyscrapers, you'll love the view from the top of the London Eye.

4 If you're interested in famous people, you _____ (love) the wax figures

at Madame Tussauds.

5 You'll have fun in a boat on the lake in Hyde Park if it _____ (not be) rainy.

► Check

5 Let's go to Southend-on-Sea

Match the sentence halves.

1 If we save money, _D_   A we don't have any money.

2 If we go to Southend-on-Sea, ___   B we'll need a hot chocolate afterwards.

3 If we swim in the sea, ___   C we'll swim in the sea.

4 But we won't be able to buy hot chocolates if ___   D we'll have enough to visit Southend-on-Sea.

6 Catching a train

Write conditional sentences type 1. Add *if* and a comma if necessary.

King's Cross Station

1 you take the lift / you'll get out of the station more quickly

If you take the lift, you'll get out of the station

more quickly.

2 you'll find the platform / you follow the signs

_____

_____

3 you miss this train / there'll be another one in half an hour

_____

_____

4 you'll see the ticket office / you go left at the top of the escalator

_____

_____

5 there'll be a direct train / you wait for another seven minutes

_____

_____

6 you lose your ticket / you'll have to buy another one

_____

_____

► Check

7 See you later!

Write the conditional sentences type 1. Use the present simple and *will*-future form of the verbs.

1 we / go / shopping in Soho later if we / have / time

   We'll go shopping in Soho later if we have time.

Soho

2 they / not catch / a train if there / be / a direct bus

   _____

3 if I / finish my homework early, I / see / you in the park

   _____

4 if it / rain / later, we / wear / our rain jackets

   _____

5 if Rose / not call / at lunchtime, she / meet / us later, after school

   _____

6 we / not visit / the Science Museum if you / be / busy today

   _____

7 if you / not have / money for the cinema, I / pay / for your ticket

   _____

8 Find the mistakes

Find and correct the mistake in each sentence.

1 The app will tell us if the train ~~won't be~~ on time.

   The app will tell us if the train isn't on time.

2 If you'll find a cafe on Platform 3 if you need a drink.

   _____

3 If you open the window, will you get cold.

   _____

4 You'll need to book a window seat if you'll want to see the mountains.

   _____

5 You won't have a comfortable journey if you will sit on the table.

   _____

► Check

REVISION: Das simple past (*The simple past*)

Mit dem *simple past* sagst du, was in der Vergangenheit geschehen ist.

A **Bejahte Aussagen (*Positive statements*)**
Bei regelmäßigen Verben hängst du -*ed* an den Infinitiv des Verbs an: *jump – jumped, walk – walked*
Unregelmäßige Verben musst du auswendig lernen: *do – did, go – went, have – had*

B **Verneinte Aussagen (*Negative statements*)**
Möchtest du sagen, dass etwas nicht geschah, setzt du *didn't* vor den Infinitiv des Verbs: *didn't jump, didn't go*

C **Fragen (*Questions*)**
Bei Fragen stellst du *Did* an den Anfang der Frage. Ein Fragewort kommt noch davor.
   Did you talk to Lisa yesterday?
Where did you go on holiday last summer?   ▶ SB p. 27, p. 46, pp. 185–186, pp. 294–295

---

9 Akila's weekend in London

a) Akila and Phil are talking about their last weekend. Complete Phil's questions. Use a question word if needed.

Phil   (1) *What did you do* _____ (do) last weekend?

Akila   I went to London with my family.

Phil   Wow cool! (2) _____ (get) there? By car?

Akila   No, we drove to the train station, and then we took the train into Waterloo.

Phil   (3) _____ (see) in London?

Akila   On the first day, we saw lots of famous people. But not in real! We went to Madame Tussauds.
         On the second day we went to Notting Hill Carnival.

Phil   (4) _____ (dance) in the street?

Akila   Yes, we did. I was really tired afterwards.

Phil   (5) _____ (want) to go back home in the end?

Akila   No, I didn't. London is such an amazing city!

b) **Now complete Akila's diary entry with the simple past forms of the verbs in the box.**

- Bei Verben, die auf -*e* enden, wird nur -*d* angehängt: *arrive → arrived*
- Einige Konsonanten werden verdoppelt: *plan → planned*

be (2x) • have • listen • share • travel • ~~visit~~

On the second day in London, we (1) *visited* _____

Notting Hill Carnival. We (2) _____ to lots of great music. It (3) _____

amazing. Later we (4) _____ dinner in Covent Garden. My pizza was delicious!

I (5) _____ it with Mum. We (6) _____ tired, but happy when we

(7) _____ back home. What a wonderful weekend!   ▶ Check ⤵

10 REVISION **Tottenham play at home**

a) Makena went to see a football match. Complete her text with the simple past of the verbs in brackets.

I'm a Tottenham fan and for my birthday, my dad (1) *bought*

(buy) tickets for us to see the Tottenham vs Arsenal match on Saturday afternoon.

We (2) _____ (leave) home at 3 o'clock and we

(3) _____ (go) by bus to Acton tube station. We

(4) _____ (get) on an Elizabeth Line tube to Liverpool Street

station. We (5) _____ (have) lunch in a cafe and then we

(6) _____ (take) a train up to White Hart Lane. Tottenham has a

big new stadium with 62,850 seats! We (7)_____ (run) into the

stadium and (8) _____ (find) our seats. I (9) _____

(feel) a bit nervous because Arsenal (10) _____ (win) the last

time they played us. Luckily, we (11) _____ (be) the strongest

team this time. We (12) _____ (sing) 'Come on you Spurs!' with

the crowd and we (13) _____ (have) a brilliant time. In the end,

the score (14) _____ (be) 3–2 to Tottenham.

b) Complete Makena's statements. Use the simple past negative forms of the blue verbs.

1   We had tickets for the match on Saturday. We *didn't have* _____ tickets for the Sunday match.

2   I wore my Tottenham football shirt. I _____ an Arsenal shirt.

3   We left the house at 3 o'clock. We _____ the house at 2 o'clock.

4   We went by public transport. We _____ by car.

5   I felt nervous before the match. I _____ confident!

6   We sang 'Come on you Spurs!' We _____ 'Auld Lang Syne'.

7   Tottenham won 3–2. Arsenal _____.

▶ Check 🔁

11 Mixed grammar Party planning

a) Faith and Zoe are talking about Annabelle's party. Complete their dialogue with the words in the box.

I'll catch • I'll • I will • I wanted • will take • ~~Will you~~

Faith   (1) _Will you_____ be at Annabelle's party

        on Saturday?

Zoe   Yes, (2) _____. Will you be there?

Faith   Yes, but (3) _____ be a bit late.

Zoe   Why? What time does the party start?

Faith   At 8.30. (4) _____ to get a lift with my dad, but he's busy,

        so (5) _____ the bus instead.

Zoe   My mum (6) _____ you if you don't want to be late.

Faith   Really? Thanks.

didn't want • mum offered • I thought • won't be • won't mind • won't need

Zoe   Yeah. It's no problem. My (7) _____ to take me. She (8) _____

        if we stop at your house on the way to Annabelle's.

Faith   That would be great. I (9) _____ to ask you, but …

Zoe   It (10) _____ a problem, really.

Faith   Thank you, Zoe, now I (11) _____ to catch the bus in my party costume!

Zoe   Yeah, (12) _____ that would be uncomfortable!

b) It's the day of Annabelle's party. Find and correct one mistake in each line of the dialogue.

Zoe   ~~You will~~ be ready at 8.15 tonight? (1) _Will you_____

Faith   No, will not! I can't find my costume. (2) _____

Zoe   I'll give you a costume if you will need one. (3) _____

        I finded two really good ones yesterday. (4) _____

Faith   Really? If you have one in my size, I am careful with it. (5) _____   ▶ Check ⤵

Who we are

Erklär-film

REVISION: Die Steigerung der Adjektive mit -er / -est (The comparison of adjectives with -er/-est)

Adjektive kannst du steigern und in Vergleichen benutzen. Bei einsilbigen Adjektiven und bei zweisilbigen Adjektiven, die auf -y enden, hängst du -er / -est an das Adjektiv:

• small → smaller (Komparativ = erste Steigerungsform)	The cat is smaller than the dog.
	(Die Katze ist kleiner als der Hund.)
• tall → the tallest (Superlativ = Höchstform)	Ethan is the tallest student at school.
	(Ethan ist der größte Schüler der Schule.)

► SB p. 50, p. 75, p. 187

1 REVISION Rosie and her family

Read the sentences about Rosie and her family. Circle the correct answers.

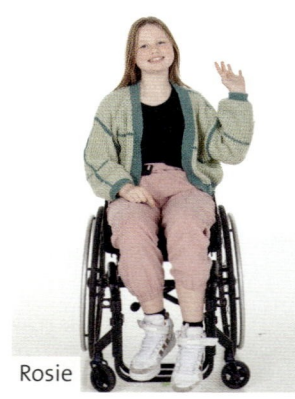

1 Rosie isn't younger / the youngest person in her family.

2 Her brother Ben is funnier / the funniest person in her family.

3 Ben has blond hair. His hair is lighter / the lightest than Rosie's.

4 Her grandad has greyer / the greyest hair in the family.

5 Rosie is always smiling. She's happier / the happiest person in the family.

Rosie

2 REVISION Omar's family

Complete the description of Omar's family. Use the comparative or superlative form of the adjectives.

Omar lives with his parents and his (1) *younger* (young) brother

and sister, Malik and Aaliyah. His mum is Dana and she is

Omar's family

(2) _____ (old) person in Omar's family. Dana is one year (3) _____ (old)

than Omar's father, Rasheed. Rasheed is very tall. He's (4) _____ (tall) person in the

family. Aaliyah is (5) _____ (small) family member, but she has

(6) _____ (long) hair! Omar has (7) _____ (short) hair than his mum

and sister. Malik has _____ (short) hair.

► Check

REVISION: Die Steigerung der Adjektive mit *more / most* (The comparison of adjectives with more/most)

Bei längeren (vor allem dreisilbigen) Adjektiven setzt du more / most vor das Adjektiv:

- *interesting → more interesting*
  (Komparativ = erste Steigerungsform)
- *expensive → most expensive*
  (Superlativ = Höchstform)

The book is more interesting than the movie.
(Das Buch ist interessanter als der Film.)
The most expensive cities are Hongkong and Zurich.
(Die teuersten Städte sind Hongkong und Zürich.)

► SB p. 50, p. 75, p. 188

3 REVISION Talking about school

Complete the conversations. Use the comparative or superlative form of the adjectives in brackets.

Khalif   This book is (1) _more interesting_ (interesting) than the book we read last year.

David   Cool, the teacher said it would be (2) _____ (popular) with the class.

Mum   You got 96% in your maths test. Well done! That's (3) _____ (wonderful) news I've heard all day.

Sally   But isn't it (4) _____ (important) to enjoy classes than to get high scores?

Dad   How's the new school football shirt?

Mel   It's definitely (5) _____ (comfortable) than the old football shirt.

4 Challenge Clothes shopping

Write comparatives with *and*.

1   T-shirt designs / are becoming / unusual

   T-shirt designs are becoming more and

   more unusual.

Um zu sagen, dass sich etwas stetig ändert, verwendest du *and*.
cheaper and cheaper (immer billiger)
more and more expensive (immer teurer)

2   Andrew's clothes / are getting / nice

   _____

3   Hats / are getting / old-fashioned

   _____

4   The quality of some clothes / is getting / good

   _____

► Check

Paarwörter bezeichnen Dinge, die aus zwei gleichen Teilen bestehen, z.B. Kleidungsstücke, Werkzeuge oder Brillen. Diese Wörter stehen immer im Plural. Die zugehörigen Verben, Begleiter oder Pronomen stehen ebenfalls im Plural.

These jeans *are* *very tight.* *(Diese Jeans ist sehr eng.)*
Have you seen my glasses*? I can't find* them*.* *(Hast du meine Brille gesehen? Ich kann sie nicht finden.)*
Your headphones *don't look* *cheap.* *(Deine Kopfhörer sehen nicht günstig aus.)*

Paarwörter können einen oder mehrere Gegenstände bezeichnen. Möchtest du die genaue Anzahl angeben, stellst du *a pair of* voran.

I bought a pair of scissors *yesterday.* *(Ich habe gestern eine Schere gekauft.)*
Hannah put two pairs of leggings *into her bag.* *(Hannah legte zwei Leggings in ihre Tasche.)*   ► SB p. 52

5 These jeans are nice!

Complete the sentences with the pair nouns from the box and circle the correct words.

> glasses • headphones • pyjamas • scissors • shorts • trousers

1	2	3
Those / This _____ are nice!	Where is / are my _____ ?	His _____ isn't / aren't cute.

4	5	6
Your _____ don't / doesn't look very clean.	This / These _____ look perfect on you!	I need the _____ . Do you have it / them?

6 How many jeans?

Look at the picture of Rachel's wardrobe and write how many jeans, trousers, shorts, headphones and glasses she has. Use ... *pair of*.

Rachel has _____

_____

_____

► Check ⤵

Erklär-film

Modale Hilfsverben: Erlaubnis und Verbot *(Modal verbs: permission and prohibition)*

Die meisten modalen Hilfsverben haben nur eine Form. Sie stehen im Infinitiv (in der Grundform).
- **Erlaubnis:** *I can / am allowed to play outside with the dog?* (Ich darf draußen mit dem Hund spielen?)
- **Verbot:** *Dad says I can't / mustn't / am not allowed to go to the zoo today.* (Papa sagt, ich darf heute nicht in den Zoo gehen.)
- **Höfliche Bitte:** *May / Could I have some sugar, please?* (Darf ich bitte etwas Zucker haben?)

Challenge Möchtest du über die Vergangenheit oder Zukunft sprechen, verwendest du *be (not) allowed to.*
I was allowed to stay at Ava's house after the party. (Ich durfte nach der Party bei Ava bleiben.)
I won't be allowed to go camping next summer. (Ich werde nächsten Sommer nicht zelten dürfen.)

▶ SB p. 55, p. 77, p. 188

7 What is Frank allowed to do?

Read the conversations and (circle) the correct words.

Ali   (Could) / Can't you go to the park after school?

Frank   Yes, of course, but I couldn't / mustn't come home after dark.

Ali   Are you allowed to / May you walk back on your own?

Frank   Sure because I have a phone.

Ali   And are you allowed watch / to watch TV after dinner?

Frank   Yes, I'm allowed to / mustn't watch TV for half an hour in the evenings.

8 An email to an advice column

Complete Meena's email with the phrases in the box.

'm not allowed to spend • Can we meet • can't talk • isn't allowed to have • ~~mustn't hang out~~

●●●

Dear advice column

My mum says I (1) *mustn't hang out* with my friends after school. She wants me to

come straight home every day to study. I always get good marks, and I don't understand why I

(2) _____ a bit of time with my friends. There's a bully in my class who says,

'(3) _____ after school? Oh no, I forgot – you (4) _____ to us! Hey

everyone, she (5) _____ friends!' It's horrible. What can I do?

Lonely student 😢

▶ Check

Modale Hilfsverben: Notwendigkeit, Zwang (*Modal verbs: necessity, compulsion*)

Mit *must* oder *have to / has to* sagst du, was jemand tun muss. Mit *don't have to / doesn't have to* oder *needn't* sagst du, was jemand nicht zu tun braucht.
Lukasz must / has to be home by 8.30 p.m. (Lukasz muss 20:30 Uhr zu Hause sein.)
We needn't / don't have to hurry. (Wir brauchen uns nicht zu beeilen.)

Challenge *Must* hat nur eine Form. Möchtest du etwas über die Vergangenheit oder Zukunft sagen verwendest du *have to / has to*.
I had to tidy my room yesterday. (Ich musste gestern mein Zimmer aufräumen.)
Moni will have to invite us all to her party. (Moni wird uns alle zu ihrer Party einladen müssen.)

► SB p. 55, p. 77, p. 189

9 Talking about school

Hugo is talking about what he has to do at school. Write his sentences.

1 have / to school by 8.30 a.m. / I / to get

I have to get to school by 8.30 a.m.

2 do / needn't / any homework at the weekends. / We

_____

3 wear / have / We / a uniform with a shirt and tie. / to

_____

4 doesn't / have / to wear / My brother has already finished school, so / he / a uniform.

_____

5 black shoes and they / have / We / to wear / must be / clean.

_____

10 What does that sign mean?

Look at the signs and complete the instructions.
Use *don't have to, must* or *mustn't* with the verbs in the box.

eat • lock • put rubbish • ~~take photos~~ • talk • wear

1 You *don't have to take photos*, but you can if you want to.

2 You _____ here.

3 You _____ in the bin. Let's keep our park clean!

4 You _____ your bike here, but you can if you want to.

5 You _____ in the library.

6 You _____ a helmet.

► Check

Erklär-film

Modale Hilfsverben: Fähigkeit *(Modal verbs: ability)*

Möchtest du sagen, dass jemand etwas tun oder nicht tun **kann**, verwendest du *can / can't* oder *be (not) able to*.
Penguins *can / are able to* swim, but they *can't / aren't able to* fly.
(Pinguine können schwimmen, aber sie können nicht fliegen.)

Challenge *Be (not) able to* hat auch Vergangenheits- und Zukunftsformen.
My mum was able to dance well when she was young. (Meine Mutter konnte gut tanzen, als sie jung war.)
You'll be able to speak English soon. (Du wirst bald Englisch sprechen können.) ▶ SB p. 77, p. 189

---

11 Fast fashion

Circle the correct words. Always two options are correct.

Fast fashion is a business model, so businesses **don't have to** / **are able to** / **can**
make and sell new clothes quickly. That way they **can** / **need** / **are able to** make
a lot of money. People think they **can't** / **aren't able to** / **must** wear clothes
if they are out of trend and they throw them away.
The opposite of fast fashion is slow fashion. It focuses on slow
production times and quality, and you are **able to** / **can** / **mustn't** wear these
clothes for a long time. Remember! You don't have to throw away a piece of
clothing just because you think it isn't trendy any longer. You **can** / **are able to** / **needn't** wear it with
something special to create an attractive outfit. It's good for our planet!

---

12 Mike's fashion

Mike is talking about his clothes. Complete his sentences with the phrases from the box.

| are able to • aren't able • can always • can borrow • can save • I can't |

I like fashion and I like to wear trendy clothes. But my parents don't give me much

pocket money, so (1) _____ buy expensive clothes. That's OK. I

(2) _____ go to charity shops or second-hand shops to look for cool

things. And I (3) _____ from my brother! We're the same size, so we

(4) _____ share our clothes. That way we (5) _____ a

lot of money. The only problem is that we (6) _____ to swap shoes.

My brother's feet are big, a lot bigger than my feet.

▶ Check 🔖

Modale Hilfsverben: Möglichkeit und Rat (Modal verbs: possibility and advice)

May, might und *could* verwendest du, wenn du sagen möchtest, dass etwas möglich ist.
It *may* *be sunny tomorrow. (Es könnte morgen sonnig sein. / Vielleicht ist es morgen sonnig.)*
This *could be* *a way out. (Das könnte ein Ausweg sein.)*
They *might* *get their first child soon. (Sie werden / könnten vielleicht bald ihr erstes Kind bekommen.)*

Möchtest du jemandem einen Rat geben, verwendest du *should* oder *shouldn't*.
You *should* *take your umbrella – it's rainy outside. (Du solltest deinen Regenschirm mitnehmen – draußen regnet es.)*
You *shouldn't* *eat so much chocolate and cake. (Du solltest nicht so viel Schokolade und Kuchen essen.)*

► SB pp. 56–57, p. 189

13 Talking about the fashion show

Write the sentences with the missing modal verbs in the correct place.

1 all the tickets / I think / for the fashion show / we / sell (might)

I think we might sell all the tickets for the fashion show.

2 we / go / tonight / to the fashion show (may)

_____

3 make a speech / Jonnie / after the show (could)

_____

4 there / this evening / a lot of people there / be (might)

_____

5 to arrive early / try / we (should)

_____

6 some new clothes / I / to the show / bring (could)

_____

7 to the show / my parents / after dinner / come (may)

_____

8 photos / you / without permission / take (shouldn't)

_____

► Check

Reflexivpronomen und *each other (Reflexive pronouns and each other)*

A Mit Reflexivpronomen sagst du, dass jemand etwas **selbst** tut. Sie enden auf *-self/-selves*.
Für jede Person gibt es eine eigene Form, die du lernen musst.

I enjoy myself.	*We enjoy ourselves.*
You enjoy yourself.	*You enjoy yourselves.*
He enjoys himself.	*They enjoy themselves.*
She enjoys herself.	
It enjoys itself.	

B Möchtest du sagen, dass Menschen etwas **gegenseitig** tun, verwendest du *each other*.
We like each other a lot. (Wir mögen uns (gegenseitig) sehr.)

! Vergleiche:

Emma and Jana took photos of themselves. (= Emma und Jana haben Fotos gemacht, auf denen sie zusammen zu sehen sind.)	*Emma and Jana took photos of each other.* (= Emma hat Fotos von Jana gemacht, und Jana hat Fotos von Emma gemacht. Sie haben sich gegenseitig fotografiert.) ▶ SB p. 58, p. 190

---

14 Matching

Match the sentences halves.

1 Omar took these photos _D_	A myself. Do you like them?
2 I made these clothes ___	B yourselves clothes that you can wear for a long time.
3 We enjoyed ___	C ourselves at the art show.
4 Tina and Max bought ___	D himself, walking around the streets of Manchester.
5 You should get ___	E herself how to design clothes.
6 Carina has taught ___	F themselves some new clothes to go out in.

---

15 Themselves or each other

Look at the pictures and the ⃝circle the correct words.

The students are taking a photo of themselves / each other.

Li and her grandma are smiling at each other / themselves.

Gina and Anton aren't talking to themselves / each other.

Hugo and his dad are looking at each other / themselves.

▶ Check

16 Family and friends

Complete the sentences with reflexive pronouns.

1 Would you like to try some cake? I made it *myself*_____!

2 Read this poem, it's really good. Mei wrote it _____ .

3 Did you and Lara make _____ some party outfits?

4 Don't worry about my brothers. They can take care of _____ .

5 I hate the rain. I wish the dog could walk _____ .

6 I have confidence in you, Ali. You should have confidence in _____ too.

7 Don't worry about Tommo, he often spends time by _____ . He likes it.

8 No one was in the kitchen, so we helped _____ to some cheese.

17 Talking about a friend

Complete the conversation with the words from the box.

| each other (2x) • myself • ourselves • yourself • ~~yourselves~~ |

Merke dir diese Ausdrücke:
Help yourself. (Greif zu. / Bediene dich.)
Enjoy yourself! (Viel Spaß!)

Aura   Did you and Jordan enjoy (1) *yourselves*_____ when you went out together

at the weekend?

Andrzej   Yes, Jordan and I always enjoy (2) _____ when we go out!

Aura   And do you really share the same birthday?

Andrzej   Yes, we do. And this year we actually bought (3) _____ the same present!

Aura   Oh, no! What did you give (4) _____ ?

Andrzej   This yellow hat. Do you like it?

Aura   It's cool, I'd like to get one for (5) _____

as well.

Andrzej   You can borrow mine. Help (6) _____ !

 ► Check

18 MIXED GRAMMAR Visit Manchester

Read the advert for Manchester and (circle) the correct words or phrases.

Visit Manchester

Everyone (should) / doesn't have to visit Manchester.
It's the largest / the most large city in the north and
the third biggest in the UK, after London and Birmingham.
And it has the warmest / the most warm welcome of any
British city.

- Are you into culture? Enjoy each other / yourself
  in the city's museums – there are five big museums
  to choose from.

- Fashion fans! Take yourselves / themselves to the Northern Quarter, where there are lots of
  trendy clothes stores.

- Do you like music? There's nowhere cooler / more cool than the independent music shops
  around Oldham Street.

- Football fans are able to / are allowed to see the Etihad Stadium, the home of Manchester City
  FC, or you can / needn't visit Manchester United FC's stadium, Old Trafford.

Manchester is a city that's very proud of itself / themselves. Many visitors say it might / mustn't be
the most exciting city in the UK!

19 MIXED GRAMMAR What we can do

Complete the sentences with the verbs in the box.

> can speak • can't speak • 's able to play • isn't able to get into • can't find • 's able to help

1 We _____ our tickets for the concert.

2 I _____ English, but I _____ French.

3 Luckily, my mum is good at science and she _____ me with my

homework.

4 My dad is very musical. He _____ three instruments.

5 My sister practises a lot on her guitar, but she _____ the school band.

► Check

REVISION: Adverbien der Art und Weise *(Adverbs of manner)* ▶

Erklär-
film

Adverbien der Art und Weise beschreiben, wie du etwas tust oder wie etwas geschieht. Sie beziehen sich auf ein Verb. Die meisten Adverbien bildest du durch Anfügen von *-ly* an ein Adjektiv.

Adjektiv	Adverb	
clear	*clearly*	*Mila speaks slowly and clearly.*
slow	*slowly*	*(Mila spricht langsam und deutlich.)*

Manchmal gibt es Unregelmäßigkeiten bei der Schreibung oder Sonderformen:

angry → angrily	*good → well*	*Clara speaks German very well.*
happy → happily	*fast → fast*	*Andrew can run very fast.*
full → fully	*hard → hard*	*Jonathan worked hard.*

▶ SB p. 84, p. 190

---

1 REVISION **Adverb or adjective?**

Read the sentences and ⟨circle⟩ the correct words.

Nach *be* steht immer ein Adjektiv:
That film was amazing!

1 Your sister is very ⟨chatty⟩ / chattily today!

2 My cousin dressed trendy / trendily for his birthday party.

3 I was riding my bike slow / slowly.

4 We ate in a traditional / traditionally Indian restaurant.

5 Our teacher explained the answers clear / clearly.

---

2 REVISION **A ghost story**

Complete Tommo's ghost story with the adverb form of the adjectives in brackets.

Someone knocked (1) _____ (loud) on the door. It was strange because no one lived

here – the house was empty. Then someone knocked (2) _____ (hard) again. I looked

at my friends (3) _____ (nervous). We stood (4) _____ (quiet) and

watched the door. The door opened (5) _____ (slow) and a white figure moved

(6) _____ (silent) into the room. Suddenly, my friends ran (7) _____ (fast)

to the front door and out of the house. But I couldn't move ...

▶ Check

3 REVISION **Looking for Nessie**

Complete the sentences with the adverbs.

carefully • differently • officially • ~~peacefully~~ • slowly

---

www.whatisnessie.example.com

In 1934, someone took a photo of something swimming (1) *peacefully* across

Loch Ness. People thought it was a 'sea monster', but no one could identify the creature

(2) _____. They looked for Nessie

(3) _____ and (4) _____.

But after many days, they didn't see anything.

Now, 90 years later, scientists are looking for the Loch Ness

Monster again. But this time, they're doing it (5) _____ . They're using modern

technique like drones and scanners to find the monster. Will they be successful?

---

4 REVISION **How did they do it?**

Write sentences. Use the adverb form of the adjectives.

Adverbs of manner stehen in der Regel nach dem Verb. Gibt es aber ein Objekt im Satz, stehen sie nach dem Objekt.

1   angry / at his brother / Ahmed shouted

   Ahmed shouted angrily at his brother.

2   my cousins sang / at the festival / beautiful

   _____

3   for the old lady / Frank opened the door / polite

   _____

4   scary / a ghost screamed / in the film

   _____

5   uncle Shaun laughed / at the TV show / happy

   _____

▶ Check ⬎

5 Adjectives after state verbs

a) Look at the verbs in the sentences in b. Highlight them in blue if they describe a state[1] and in red if they describe an action.

b) Circle the correct words.

1 The ghost in this film looks crazy / crazily.

2 Our plane landed safe / safely at 6.30 p.m.

3 This burger tastes amazing / amazingly.

4 Josh sat unhappy / unhappily in his chair.

5 The school is becoming green / greenly.

6 You must speak nice / nicely to your teacher.

7 I'm not sure this is right. I don't feel positive / positively about it.

c) Write the sentences with the correct adverb or adjective forms.

1 those new jeans look / uncomfortable

Those new jeans look uncomfortable.

2 dinner smells / amazing

_____

3 Natasha played that song / perfect

_____

4 the new Studio Ghibli film sounds / good

_____

5 our new teacher treats us / strict

_____

6 does your apple taste / nice / ?

_____

► Check

[1] **state** *der Zustand*

Adverbien kannst du ebenso wie Adjektive steigern und in Vergleichen benutzen.
Bei *-ly*-Adverbien bildest du die erste Steigerungsform (Komparativ) mit *more* und die Höchstform (Superlativ) mit *most* vor dem Adverb.

Bei kurzen (meist einsilbigen) Adverbien hängst du *-er* für den Komparativ und *-est* für den Superlativ an das Adverb.

Merke dir diese Ausnahmen:
• well → *better* → *(the) best*
• badly → *worse* → *(the) worst*

Could you please drive more carefully?
(Könntest du bitte vorsichtiger fahren?)
The old Lady walks more slowly than her dog.
(Die alte Dame geht langsamer als ihr Hund.)
Who dances (the) most beautifully?
(Wer tanzt am schönsten?)

My brother can run faster than me.
(Mein Bruder kann schneller rennen als ich.)
Grandpa speaks the loudest at Christmas dinner.
(Opa spricht beim Weihnachtsessen am lautesten.)

Fatima plays football better than her brother.
(Fatima spielt besser Fußball als ihr Bruder.)

▶ SB p. 111, p. 191

6 Challenge Comparative and superlative adverbs

Complete the table.

adverb	comparative	superlative
beautifully	more beautifully	
hard		the hardest
	more dangerously	
quietly		
		the fastest
	worse	

7 Challenge They do things better

Complete the sentences with the comparative form of the adverbs in brackets.

1 My little sister won the chess match. She played

   <u>more cleverly</u> (clever) than me.

2 Holly read her email _____ (careful) than usual.

   She didn't want to make any mistakes.

3 My mum and dad speak good English, but my aunt speaks it

   even _____ (good).

4 To get good marks, I'm going to study _____ (hard) than last year.

5 I was nervous, so I began to speak _____ (quick).

▶ Check 🔁

8 [Challenge] The things they do best

Follow the lines to find out how the people do the things. Then complete the sentences with the superlative form of the adverbs.

1 *As It Was* is the song Mike sings _____ .

2 Lea swam the _____ today and came last in the

   competition.

3 Of all my students, Bianca plays the trumpet the _____ .

4 Everyone was sad about the news, but Noah looked at me

   the _____ .

5 Ben and Steve eat a lot and they eat the _____ too.

6 'Can I help you?' asked the girl the _____ .

quiet

fast

good

bad

slow

sad

9 [Challenge] What a match!

Read Ida's article about the school team's football match. Circle the correct adverb forms.

What a match!

Today our school football team played the most important match of the season. And did they play amazingly / more amazingly? – Oh yes, they did.

The team came nervously / nervous onto the football field. I think they waited for the start of the match more nervously / the most nervously than ever before. Zoha and Paadina played well / better today. They played better / the best at the beginning of the second half when Paadina moved the ball calm / calmly to Zoha and Zoha scored a goal. The team and the audience cheered happily / more happily. Our team won 3-1!

After the match, I asked Sara how she liked to play in today's match. She said 'I was so worried that I think I played bad / badly. I played worse / the worst than last week.' But Sara is wrong! 'Sara ran fast / faster today. She hit the balls harder / the hardest and played more wonderfully / the most wonderfully than in all the other matches.' said Coach Kent.

► Check

Erklär-film

REVISION: Das present perfect: Bejahte und verneinte Aussagesätze *(Positive and negative statements)*

Mit dem *present perfect* sagst du, dass jemand etwas gemacht oder nicht gemacht hat. Der genaue Zeitpunkt ist unwichtig oder unbekannt und wird nicht genannt.
Es besteht aus zwei Teilen: *have / has + past participle* des Verbs.

A **Bejahte Aussagesätze**		B **Verneinte Aussagesätze**	
I You We They	*have worked* all day. *'ve sent* an email.	I You We They	*have not worked* all day. *haven't sent* an email.
He/She/It	*has worked* all day. *'s sent* an email.	He/She/It	*has not worked* all day *hasn't sent* an email.

Beachte bei der Bildung des *past participle*:
• Bei regelmäßigen Verben hängst du *-ed* an das Verb: *jump → jumped*.
• Bei Verben, die auf *-e* enden, wird nur *-d* angehängt: *arrive → arrived*.
• Einige Verben haben unregelmäßige Formen. Diese musst du lernen.

► SB p. 87, p. 192, pp. 294–295

---

10 REVISION Talking about experiences

Read about the people's experiences. Circle the correct signal words.

1 Vicente and Lena are very excited. They've ever / (never) been to the UK before.

2 Akila has just / never won the best player prize. Congratulations, Akila!

3 My family and I have flown once / twice. Both times we flew to Poland.

4 You haven't met my cousins already / yet. Let's go and meet them.

5 Have you watched a film all in English? – No, not ever / yet.

6 I love Austria, I've already / just been there three times.

---

11 REVISION A music festival

Write the sentences. Use the positive or negative present perfect form of the verbs.

Die Kurzform von *have* ist *'ve*:
I have tried = I've tried.

1 *The concert has started, but the band hasn't played my favourite song yet.*
The concert / start / but the band / not play / my favourite song yet.

2 _____
The first band / finish / and they / walk / off the stage.

3 _____
Laura / go / to the stage but her brothers / not go / with her.

4 _____
Marc / lose / his friends and his phone / break.

► Check

REVISION: Das present perfect: Fragen und Antworten *(Questions and answers)*

In Fragen vertauschst du das Subjekt und *have / has*:

it has → has it?

*Has the movie started yet? – Yes, it has. / No, it hasn't.
Where has she been? – She has been at the library.*

▶ SB p. 87, p. 193

12 REVISION **Let's have an adventure!**

a) **Write the words in the correct order to form present perfect questions.**

1 *Has anyone you know ever jumped from a cliff?*
   anyone you know / from a cliff? / jumped / has / ever

2 _____
   climbed / you / ever / a mountain? / have

3 _____
   what / have / you / had / for your picnic?

4 _____
   skiing before? / has / been / your best friend

5 _____
   where / your bike? / you / have / left

6 _____
   forgotten / have / you / your surfboard? / why

b) **Write present perfect questions.**

1 *What animals have you seen in the mountains?*
   what animals / you / see / in the mountains?

2 _____
   you / see / any goats?

3 _____
   where / you / be / ?

4 _____
   the tour guide / arrive / yet?

5 _____
   how high / you / climb / ?

6 _____
   you / walk / 15 km?

7 _____
   who / you / hike / with?

8 _____
   why / you / buy / new sunglasses?

▶ Check ⬎

ADVANCED

lighthouse 3

Grammarmaster

Lösungen

Cornelsen

1 Revision Pearl's journey from Covent Garden to Camden Market

1 will meet • **2** won't/will not take • **3** won't/will not go • **4** 'll/will walk • **5** 'll/will catch

Alle Lösungen aus diesem Heft findest du auch in deiner Cornelsen Lernen App.

2 Revision Decisions, offers and other situations

1 We won't play football today.
2 I'll/will help you to find it.
3 I won't/will not get more than 75 %.
4 I think it'll/will be sunny later.

3 Revision A trip to London

a) b)

1 Will Omar visit Big Ben? – Yes, he will.
2 Will Grace go on the Orbit Slide? – No, she won't / will not.
3 Will Dylan and Omar look at the graffiti in the Leake Street Tunnel? – Yes, they will.
4 Will Grace and Omar go the South Bank? – Yes, they will.
5 Will Omar have a ride on the London Eye? – No, he won't / will not.
6 Will Grace and Dylan visit the Houses of Parliament? – No, they won't / will not.

4 Advice for visitors to London

a)

1 If you go to Trafalgar Square, you**'ll see** Nelson's Column.
2 You**'ll go** past the London Eye if you walk along the South Bank.
3 If you **don't join** the Ghost Bus tour, you'll miss all the scary stories!
4 If you buy your tube ticket with a credit card, you**'ll save** money.
5 You'll be able to use public transport all day if you have a Travelcard.
6 If you **don't have** any money, you'll be able to get into most museums – lots of them are free.

b)

1 If you go by bus, you**'ll get** a good view of London from the top of a double-decker.
2 You'll see some famous black birds called 'ravens' if you **visit** the Tower of London.
3 If you **like** skyscrapers, you'll love the view from the top of the London Eye.
4 If you're interested in famous people, you**'ll / will love** the wax figures at Madame Tussauds.
5 You'll have fun in a boat on the lake in Hyde Park if it **isn't / 's not / is not** rainy.

5 Let's go to Southend-on-Sea

1 D • **2** C • **3** B • **4** A

6 Catching a train

1 If you take the lift, you'll get out of the station more quickly.
2 You'll find the platform if you follow the signs.
3 If you miss this train, there'll be another one in half an hour.
4 You'll see the ticket office if you go left at the top of the escalator.
5 There'll be a direct train if you wait for another seven minutes.
6 If you lose your ticket, you'll have to buy another one.

7 See you later!

1 We'll go shopping in Soho later if we have time.
2 They won't / will not catch a train if there's a direct bus.
3 If I finish my homework early, I'll / will see you in the park.
4 If it rains later, we'll / will wear our rain jackets.
5 If Rose doesn't / does not call us at lunchtime, she'll / will meet us later, after school.
6 We won't / will not visit the Science Museum if you're / are busy today.
7 If you don't / do not have money for the cinema, I'll / will pay for your ticket.

8 Find the mistakes

1 The app will tell us if the train **isn't** on time.
2 **You'll** find a cafe on Platform 3 if you need a drink.
3 If you open the window, you **will** get cold.
4 You'll need to book a window seat if **you want** to see the mountains.
5 You won't have a comfortable journey if you **sit** on the table.

9 REVISION Akila's weekend in London

a)
1 What did you do
2 How did you get
3 What did you see
4 Did you dance
5 Did you want

b)
1 visited · 2 listened · 3 was · 4 had · 5 shared · 6 were · 7 travelled

10 REVISION Tottenham play at home

a)
1 bought · 2 left · 3 went · 4 got · 5 had · 6 took · 7 ran · 8 found · 9 felt · 10 won ·
11 were · 12 sang · 13 had · 14 was

b)
1 didn't have · 2 didn't / did not wear · 3 didn't / did not leave · 4 didn't / did not go ·
5 didn't / did not feel · 6 didn't / did not sing · 7 didn't / did not win

11 MIXED GRAMMAR Party planning

a)

Faith	**Will you** be at Annabelle's party on Saturday?
Zoe	Yes, **I will**. Will you be there?
Faith	Yes, but **I will** be a bit late.
Zoe	Why? What time does the party start?
Faith	At 8.30. **I wanted** to get a lift with my dad but he's busy, so **I'll catch** the bus instead.
Zoe	My mum **will take** you if you don't want to be late.
Faith	Really? Thanks.
Zoe	Yeah. It's no problem. My **mum offered** to take me. She **won't mind** if we stop at your house on the way to Annabelle's.
Faith	That would be great. I **didn't want** to ask you, but …
Zoe	It **won't be** a problem, really.
Faith	Thank you, Zoe, now I **won't need** to catch the bus in my party costume!
Zoe	Yeah, **I thought** that would be uncomfortable!

b)

Zoe	**Will you** be ready at 8.15 tonight?
Faith	No, **I** will not! I can't find my costume.
Zoe	I'll give you a costume if you **need** one.
	I **found** two really good ones yesterday.
Faith	Really? If you have one in my size, **I'll / will be** careful with it.

Unit 2 Manchester: Who we are

1 REVISION Rosie and her family

1 Rosie isn't **the youngest** person in her family.
2 Her brother Ben **the funniest** person in her family.
3 Ben has blond hair. His hair is **lighter** than Rosie's.
4 Her grandad has **the greyest** hair in the family.
5 Rosie is always smiling. She's **the happiest** person in the family.

2 REVISION Omar's family

Omar lives with his parents and his **younger** brother and sister, Malik and Aaliyah. His mum is Dana and she is **the oldest** person in Omar's family. Dana is one year **older** than Omar's father, Rasheed. Rasheed is very tall. He's **the tallest** person in the family. Aaliyah is **the smallest** family member, but she has **the longest** hair! Omar has **shorter** hair than his mum and sister. Malik has **the shortest** hair.

3 REVISION Talking about school

1 more interesting
2 more popular
3 the most wonderful
4 more important
5 more comfortable

4 Challenge Clothes shopping

1 T-shirt designs are becoming more and more unusual.
2 Andrew's clothes are getting nicer and nicer.
3 Hats are getting more and more old-fashioned.
4 The quality of some clothes is getting better and better.

5 These jeans are nice!

1 **Those pyjamas** are nice!
2 Where **are** my **headphones**?
3 His **shorts aren't** cute.
4 Your **glasses don't** look very clean.
5 **These trousers** look perfect on you!
6 I need the **scissors**. Do you have **them**?

6 How many jeans?

Rachel has three pairs of jeans, four pairs of trousers, three pairs of glasses and one pair of headphones.

7 What is Frank allowed to do?

Ali   **Could** you go to the park after school?

Frank   Yes, of course, but I **mustn't** come home after dark.

Ali   **Are you allowed to** walk back on your own?

Frank   Sure because I have a phone.

Ali   And are you allowed **to watch** TV after dinner?

Frank   Yes, I**'m allowed to** watch TV for half an hour in the evenings.

8 An email to an advice column

Dear advice column

My mum says I **mustn't hang out** with my friends after school. She wants me to come straight home every day to study. I always get good marks, and I don't understand why I**'m not allowed to spend** a bit of time with my friends. There's a bully in my class who says, '**Can we meet** after school? Oh no, I forgot – you **can't talk** to us! Hey everyone, she **isn't allowed to have** friends!' It's horrible. What can I do?

Lonely student

9 Talking about school

1   I have to get to school by 8.30 a.m.

2   We needn't do any homework at the weekends.

3   We have to wear a uniform with a shirt and tie.

4   My brother has already finished school, so he doesn't have to wear a uniform.

5   We have to wear black shoes and they must be clean.

10 What does that sign mean?

1   You **don't have to take photos**, but you can if you want to.

2   You **mustn't eat** here.

3   You **have to put rubbish** in the bin. Let's keep our park clean!

4   You **don't have to lock** your bike here, but you can if you want to.

5   You **mustn't** talk in the library.

6   You **have to** a helmet.

11 Fast fashion

Fast fashion is a business model, so businesses **are able to / can** make and sell new clothes quickly. That way they **can / are able to** make a lot of money. People think they **can't / aren't able to** wear clothes if they are out of trend and they throw them away.

The opposite of fast fashion is slow fashion. It focuses on slow production times and quality, and you are **able to / can** wear these clothes for a long time. Remember! You don't have to throw away a piece of clothing just because you think it isn't trendy any longer. You **can / are able to** wear it with something special to create an attractive outfit. It's good for our planet!

12 Mike's fashion

I like fashion and I like to wear trendy clothes. But my parents don't give me much pocket money, so **I can't** buy expensive clothes. That's OK. I **can always** go to charity shops or second-hand shops to look for cool things. And I **can borrow** from my brother! We're the same size, so we **are able to** share our clothes. That way we **can save** a lot of money. The only problem is that we **aren't able** to swap shoes. My brother's feet are big, a lot bigger than my feet.

13 Talking about the fashion show

1 I think we might sell all the tickets for the fashion show.
2 We may go to the fashion show tonight.
3 Jonnie could make a speech after the show.
4 There might be a lot of people there this evening.
5 We should try to arrive early.
6 I could bring some new clothes to the show.
7 My parents may come to the show after dinner.
8 You shouldn't take photos without permission.

14 Matching

1 D · **2** A · **3** C · **4** F · **5** B · **6** E

15 Themselves or each other

1 The students are taking photo of **themselves**.
2 Li and her grandma are smiling at **each other**.
3 Gina and Anton aren't talking to **each other**.
4 Hugo and his dad are looking at **themselves**.

16 Family and friends

1 Would you like to try some cake? I made it **myself**!
2 Read this poem, it's really good. Mei wrote it **herself**.
3 Did you and Lara make **yourselves** some party outfits?
4 Don't worry about my brothers. They can take care of **themselves**.
5 I hate the rain. I wish the dog could walk **itself**.
6 I have confidence in you, Ali. You should have confidence in **yourself** too.
7 Don't worry about Tommo, he often spends time by **himself**. He likes it.
8 No one was in the kitchen, so we helped **ourselves** to some cheese.

17 Talking about a friend

Aura   Did you and Jordan enjoy **yourselves** when you went out together at the weekend?
Andrzej   Yes, Jordan and I always enjoy **ourselves** when we go out!
Aura   And do you really share the same birthday?
Andrzej   Yes, we do. And this year we actually bought **each other** the same present!
Aura   Oh, no! What did you give **each other**?
Andrzej   This yellow hat. Do you like it?
Aura   It's cool, I'd like to get one for **myself** as well.
Andrzej   You can borrow mine. Help **yourself**!

18 MIXED GRAMMAR Visit Manchester

Everyone **should** visit Manchester. It's **the largest** city in the north and the third biggest in the UK, after London and Birmingham. And it has **the warmest** welcome of any British city.

- Are you into culture? Enjoy **yourself** in the city's museums – there are five big museums to choose from.
- Fashion fans! Take **yourselves** to the Northern Quarter, where there are lots of trendy clothes stores.
- Do you like music? There's nowhere **cooler** than the independent music shops around Oldham Street.
- Football fans **are able to** see the Etihad Stadium, the home of Manchester City FC, or you **can** visit Manchester United FC's stadium, Old Trafford.

Manchester is a city that's very proud of **itself**. Many visitors say it **might** be the most exciting city in the UK!

19 MIXED GRAMMAR What we can do

1 We **can't find** our tickets for the concert.
2 I **can speak** English, but I **can't speak** French. / I **can't speak** English, but I **can speak** French.
3 Luckily, my mum is good at science and she**'s able to help** me with my homework.
4 My dad is very musical. He**'s able to play** three instruments.
5 My sister practises a lot on her guitar, but she **isn't able to get into** the school band.

Unit 3 Scotland: Adventure

1 REVISION Adverb or adjective?

1 Your sister is very **chatty** today!
2 My cousin dressed **trendily** for his birthday party.
3 I was riding my bike **slowly**.
4 We ate in a **traditional** Indian restaurant.
5 Our teacher explained the answers **clearly**.

2 REVISION A ghost story

Someone knocked **loudly** on the door. It was strange because no one lived here – the house was empty. Then someone knocked **hard** again. I looked at my friends **nervously**. We stood **quietly** and watched the door. The door opened **slowly** and a white figure moved **silently** into the room. Suddenly, my friends ran **fast** to the front door and out of the house. But I couldn't move …

3 REVISION Looking for Nessie

In 1934, someone took a photo of something swimming **peacefully** across Loch Ness. People thought it was a 'sea monster', but no one could identify the creature **officially**. They looked for Nessie **slowly** and **carefully**. But after many days, they didn't see anything.

Now, 90 years later, scientists are looking for the Loch Ness Monster again. But this time, they're doing it **differently**. They're using modern technique like drones and scanners to find the monster. Will they be successful?

4 REVISION **How did they do it?**

1. Ahmed shouted angrily at his brother.
2. My cousins sang beautifully at the festival.
3. Frank opened the door politely for the old lady.
4. A ghost screamed scarily in the film.
5. Uncle Shaun laughed happily at the TV show.

5 Adjectives after state verbs

a) b)

1. The ghost in this film looks **crazy**.
2. Our plane landed **safely** at 6.30. p.m.
3. This burger tastes **amazing**.
4. Josh sat **unhappily** in his chair.
5. The school is becoming **green**.
6. You must speak **nicely** to your teacher.
7. I'm not sure this is right. I don't feel **positive** about it.

c)

1. Those new jeans look uncomfortable.
2. Dinner smells amazing.
3. Natasha played that song perfectly.
4. The new Studio Ghibli film sounds good.
5. Our new teacher treats us strictly.
6. Does your apple taste nice?

6 Challenge **Comparative and superlative adverbs**

adverb	comparative	superlative
beautifully	more beautifully	*the most beautifully*
hard	*harder*	the hardest
dangerously	more dangerously	*the most dangerously*
quietly	*more quietly*	*the most quietly*
fast	*faster*	the fastest
badly	worse	*the worst*

7 Challenge **They do things better**

1. My little sister won the chess match. She played **more cleverly** than me.
2. Holly read her email **more carefully** than usual. She didn't want to make any mistakes.
3. My mum and dad speak good English, but my aunt speaks it even **better**.
4. To get good marks, I'm going to study **harder** than last year.
5. I was nervous, so I began to speak **more quickly**.

8 Challenge **The things they do best**

1. *As It Was* is the song Mike sings **best**.
2. Lea swam the **most slowly** today and came last in the competition.
3. Of all my students, Biance plays the trumpet the **worst**.
4. Everyone was sad about the news, but Noah looked at me the **saddest**.
5. Ben and Steve eat a lot and they eat the **fastest** too.
6. 'Can I help you?' asked the girl the **most quietly**.

9 `Challenge` What a match!

Today our school football team played the most important match of the season. And did they play **amazingly**? – Oh yes, they did.

The team came **nervously** onto the football field. I think they waited for the start of the match **more nervously** than ever before. Zoha and Paadina played **well** today. They played **the best** at the beginning of the second half when Paadina moved the ball **calmly** to Zoha and Zoha scored a goal. The team and the audience cheered **happily**. Our team won 3-1!

After the match, I asked Sara how she liked to play in today's match. She said 'I was so worried that I think I played **badly**. I played **worse** than last week.' But Sara is wrong! 'Sara ran **fast** today. She hit the balls **harder** and played **more wonderfully** than in all the other matches.' said Coach Kent.

10 REVISION Talking about experiences

1 Vicente and Lena are very excited. They've **never** been to the UK before.
2 Akila has **just** won the best player prize. Congratulations, Akila!
3 My family and I have flown **twice**. Both times we flew to Poland.
4 You haven't met my cousins **yet**. Let's go and meet them.
5 Have you watched a film all in English? – No, not **yet**.
6 I love Austria, I've **already** been there three times.

11 REVISION A music festival

1 The concert has started, but the band hasn't played my favourite song yet.
2 The first band has finished and they've / have walked off the stage.
3 Laura has gone to the stage, but her brothers haven't gone with her.
4 Marc has lost his friends and his phone has broken.

12 REVISION Let's have an adventure!

a)
1 Has anyone you know ever jumped from a cliff?
2 Have you ever climbed a mountain?
3 What have you had for your picnic?
4 Has your best friend been skiing before?
5 Where have you left your bike?
6 Why have you forgotten your surfboard?

b)
1 What animals have you seen in the mountains?
2 Have you seen any goats?
3 Where have you been?
4 Has the tour guide arrived yet?
5 How high have you climbed?
6 Have you walked 15 km?
7 Who have you hiked with?
8 Why have you bought new sunglasses?

13 Since or for?

since	for
since 2023	for a long time
since I was ten	for a month
since last weekend	for hours
since yesterday	for two years

14 Facts about Scotland

Until the seventeenth century, England and Scotland were independent. But the two countries have been one 'kingdom' **since** 1603, **for** more than 400 years. The oldest tree in Europe is in Scotland. It has been alive **for** 3,000 years! Edinburgh has been the capital of Scotland **since** 1437. Glasgow, the biggest city in Scotland, has the third oldest underground in the world. It has been in use **since** 1896. Saint Valentine died on 14th February 269 AD in Glasgow. His grave has been in the city **for** more than 1,750 years.

15 How long?

1 We haven't watched a film since we went to London.
2 I've / have played tennis since I was five.
3 They've / have read books in the library for half an hour.
4 We've / have had a dog for two months.
5 He's / has had the same piano teacher for many years.

16 Challenge An interview with your English exchange partner

a)
1 How long have you been at your school?
2 How long have you lived in your home?
3 What's your favourite sport? How long have you played it?
4 What's your favourite computer game? How long have you liked it?
5 Who's your best friend? How long have you been friends?

b)
((Lösungsbeispiel))
1 I have been at my school since I was ten / for three years.
2 I have lived in my home since I was born / for ten months.
3 My favourite sport is football. I have played it since last summer / for five years.
4 My favourite computer game is Minecraft. I've liked it since last year / for one year.
5 My best friend is Steve. We've been friends since Year 5 / for a very long time.

17 MIXED GRAMMAR A brave teenager

1 has been
2 since
3 hard
4 harder
5 big
6 nervous
7 slowly
8 has climbed
9 for
10 has talked

1 Matching

1 B • 2 F • 3 E • 4 D • 5 A • 6 C

2 Anglesey is my favourite place

I'm making a video about the Isle of Anglesey. **My** grandparents lived there, and we spent some of **our** nicest summers on **their** farm. It was a very old house – **theirs** was the oldest house in the village. **Our** grandfather often told us the greatest ghost stories. My grandmother made Welsh cakes. **Hers** were the best! Anglesey is still my favourite place. What's **yours**?

3 Exchange partners

1 your • 2 mine • 3 yours • 4 my • 5 your • 6 its • 7 our • 8 his • 9 ours • 10 theirs • 11 their • 12 Ours

4 What's missing?

1   Is this your sister's bag? – I'm not sure, but I think it's **hers**.
2   The dog is barking because it has lost **its** toy.
3   I have a cap like that, but **yours** is nicer.
4   Ryan has a bike like that. I'm sure it's **his**.
5   Tom and Simon live in a big flat. **Theirs** is bigger than **mine**.

5 REVISION What are their plans?

a)
1   We're going to go on holiday to Wales. We aren't going to go to Spain.
2   They**'re / are going to play** rugby. They **aren't / 're not / are not going to play** football.
3   I**'m / am going to visit** Cardiff. I**'m not / am not going to visit** Anglesey.
4   She**'s / is going to sing** in Welsh. She **isn't / 's not / is not going to sing** in English.
5   He**'s / is going to do** gymnastics. He **isn't / 's not / is not going to do** judo.

b)
1   I'm going to go swimming today. I'm **not going** to wait until tomorrow!
2   We aren't going to **meet** after school. Peter **is** going to be busy today.
3   He **isn't** going to play rugby. He hates it!
4   They**'re** going to make some food now because they're hungry.
5   You're **not** going to see your dad today. **You**'re going to stay with grandma this afternoon.
6   She**'s** going to get the bus. She isn't **going** to walk.

6 REVISION Tech talk

1   Are you going to charge your phone now?
2   Is your dad going to let you get this app?
3   Are they going to connect to my Wi-Fi?
4   Are we going to click on this link?
5   Is Simon going to save the video?
6   Are you going to add captions?

7 REVISION **Digital detox**

Gwen	**Are you going to come** over to my place to play some video games?
Livia	No, I**'m / am not**. Sorry. Mum and I are going to do some digital detox.
Gwen	Oh! What **are you going to do**? Or what aren't you going to do?
Livia	Well, I'm not going to use my phone or my computer.
Gwen	**Is your mum going to use** her phone or computer?
Livia	No, she **isn't / is not**. Only if she needs to do something for her work.
Gwen	And **is your dad going to join** you too?
Livia	Yes, he **is**. Well, he wants to try at least.

8 REVISION **What are their plans for the afternoon?**

a) b)

1 Is Dylan going to play basketball? – No, he isn't.
2 Is Gwen going to play basketball? – Yes, she is.
3 Is Flynn going to listen to music? – Yes, he is.
4 Are Dylan and Owen going to make a cake? – Yes, they are.
5 Are Gwen and Flynn going to make a cake? – No, they aren't.
6 Is Gwen going to listen to music? – No, she isn't.

9 REVISION **What are you going to do this evening?**

a) b)

((Lösungsbeispiel))

Are you going to spend some time on social media? – Yes, I am. / No, I'm not.
Are you going to meet your friends? – Yes, I am. / No, I'm not.
Are you going to ask your parents to help you with your homework? – Yes, I am. / No, I'm not.

10 Challenge **What's going to happen?**

1 Manchester United are going to win the game.
2 Chris and Oliver are going to enjoy summer camp.
3 Sarah isn't / is not going to miss the bus.
4 Dario isn't / is not going to finish the test.

11 Challenge **Predictions**

((Lösungsbeispiel))

The family is going to move into the blue house. The boy is going to play football in the garden.
The children and the dog are going to have their own rooms. The children are going to play with the
dog. The parents are going to work a lot in the garden, but they're going to enjoy it. The family is
going to live happily in their new house.

12 **'Cymru' means 'Wales' in Welsh**

a)

1 'Cymry' is the adjective for people **who** are Welsh.
2 The daffodil is a flower **which** is the national symbol of Wales.
3 Rugby is the sport **which** most Welsh people love.
4 Charlotte Church is a popular singer **who** is Welsh.
5 Gareth Bale is a Welsh footballer **who** played for Real Madrid.
6 Coal mining is something **which** Wales was famous for in the past.

b)

1 C • 2 E • 3 D • 4 B • 5 F • 6 A

13 Rugby

a)

1 which · **2** which · **3** who · **4** which · **5** which · **6** who · **7** who · **8** which · **9** who

b)

1 Modern rugby comes from a game **which/that** schoolboys played at Rugby School in England in the 1820s.
2 There are at least 50 countries which have international rugby teams. ✓
3 The first international rugby match **which/that** took place was Scotland against England in 1871.
4 JPR Williams was a famous Welsh rugby player **who/that** died in 2024.
5 There are over 100 clubs in Germany **which/that** play rugby.
6 The best German teams play in the Rugby-Bundesliga which has 16 clubs. ✓

14 Green energy

1 In the past, Wales had a lot of mines which produced coal.
2 Many years ago, most Welsh people knew somebody who worked as a minor.
3 When you burn coal, it produces fumes that make climate change worse.
4 A wind turbine is a machine that uses wind energy to make electricity.
5 These are the kind of wind turbines which produce green energy.

15 Quiz time!

1 What's the name of the band **which** sang *Don't Look Back in Anger*? – **Oasis**.
2 What's the name of the man **who** wrote the lyrics of *Auld Lang Syne*? – **Robert Burnes**.
3 What's the name of the monster **which** lives in Loch Ness? – **Nessie**.
4 What's the name of a special instrument **which** they play in Scotland? – The **bagpipes**.
5 What's the title of the person **who** is the father of Prince William? – **King Charles III**.
6 What's the animal **which** you can ride on Llandudno Beach? – **Donkey**.

16 `Challenge` Cyber bullying

a)

	subject	object
1 Cyber bullying is something that 20% of teenagers have experienced.	☐	☑
2 Cyber bullying is something that we can stop if we try.	☐	☑
3 There are quite a few students who experience cyber bullying at my school.	☑	☐
4 Cyber bullying often comes from people who you know.	☐	☑
5 Some of the messages that they got were not kind.	☐	☑
6 In most countries, there are charities which help young people talk about bullying.	☑	☐

b)

Sentences 1, 2, 4, 5

c)

1 ✗
2 who
3 which
4 who
5 ✗

17 [Challenge] Digital life

a)

1 An emoji is a small picture you use to show how you're feeling.
2 A smart watch is a device which can tell you more than just the time.
3 A vlogger is a person who posts video stories online.
4 An influencer is a person you follow on social media.
5 A 'bio' is information that tells you about a person's life.
6 A filter is something you use to make a photograph look different.

b)

1 C, that • **2** A, that • **3** D • **4** F • **5** B • **6** E

18 MIXED GRAMMAR Colour by numbers

19 MIXED GRAMMAR Dylan and Owen's next video

1 Are we going to upload   A mine
2 Yes, we are.   B which
3 'm going to cut   C who
4 are going to check   D our
5 is going to be   E which
6 Are we going to add   F who
7 This is going to be   G hers
                                    H ours

1 REVISION South Voice: Orla

1 I don't know a lot about the Troubles.
2 My dad didn't / did not go to Northern Ireland last year.
3 I'm not / am not going to look at the Peace Walls.
4 We haven't / have not lived in Dublin since 2021.
5 I won't / will not be in Northern Ireland for a month.
6 My mum doesn't / does not want to go to the Titanic Belfast museum.
7 I'm not / am not looking forward to the long journey.

2 REVISION North Voice: Jack

a)
1 Where do you go to school?
2 Do you like your school?
3 What will you do after school?
4 Why did you like the North and South Voices project?
5 What are you going to do next?

b)
1 Where **do** you live?
2 Where **will** you live when you're older?
3 **Did** you go to the Giant's Causeway last week?
4 Why **do** you like the Giant's Causeway?
5 What **are** you studying at school right now?
6 **Has** that period of history been interesting?

3 REVISION Our trip to Dublin

a)
1 We wanted to stay in a B&B, **so we booked** one online.
2 We took the train to Dublin **because we don't have** a car.
3 We played card games, **so we had** something to do on the train.
4 We got into a taxi **when we arrived** at Dublin train station.
5 I looked out of the car window **while the taxi took** us to the B&B.
6 We went to our room at the B&B **after we had** a delicious dinner.

b)
1 The next morning, we went downstairs **after we had showers**.
2 ✓
3 We talked about the route **while we ate our breakfast**.
4 Then we filled our water bottles, **so we had water** for the walk.
5 But it started to rain **when we left the B&B**!
6 ✓

4 Challenge Breakfast at the B&B

a)

		simple present	present progressive
1	Jack **serves** the breakfasts (every day) during the holidays.	☑	☐
2	Jack **is serving** Orla and her mum (today)	☐	☑
3	He**'s taking** their breakfast order right (now)	☐	☑
4	Orla (never) **eats** meat.	☑	☐
5	Orla (usually) **orders** a vegetarian breakfast.	☑	☐
6	Orla's mum **is having** a full cooked breakfast (at the moment)	☐	☑

b)
1 are talking
2 wants
3 prefers
4 're / are asking
5 recommends
6 know
7 is giving
8 goes

5 Challenge Irish holiday experiences

a) b)
1   Jannis **hasn't visited** Belfast since 2023.
2   **Have you ever** visited Northern Ireland?
3   Maja **flew** to Dublin last month.
4   **Did Jack walk** on Giant's Causeway last week?
5   Nick and Sarah **didn't enjoy** the Murals tour at the weekend.
6   Alex **tried** the food on St. George's Market two days ago.
7   I **have never watched** a match at Windsor Park stadium in Belfast.
8   Yusuf **loved** his class trip to the Titanic Belfast museum yesterday.
9   Ethan **hasn't / has not sent** any postcards yet.
10 **Has** Ella **been** to Cork lots of times?

Das present perfect mit *since* oder *for* (The present perfect with *since* or *for*)

Mit dem *present perfect* sagst du auch, wie lange etwas schon andauert. Du verwendest:

- *since* um zu sagen, wann etwas begonnen hat:
  since 8 o'clock in the morning, *since* July
- *for* um zu sagen, wie lange etwas schon andauert:
  for seven months, *for* six days

They *have lived* in this country *since* 2019.
(Sie leben seit 2019 in diesem Land.)
Mila *has been* in our school *for* eight months.
(Mila ist seit acht Monaten auf unserer Schule.)
Grandma *has visited* us *for* two weeks.
(Oma hat uns zwei Wochen lang besucht.)

► SB p. 89, p. 193

13 Since or for?

Write the phrases from the box into the right list. Write them with *for* or *since*.

> ~~2023~~ • a long time • a month • hours • I was ten • last weekend • two years • yesterday

since	for
since 2023	

14 Facts about Scotland

Clara wrote about Scotland. Read her text and complete the sentences with *for* or *since*.

Scotland

Until the seventeenth century, England and Scotland were

independent. But the two countries have been one 'kingdom'

(1) _____ 1603, (2) _____ more

Edinburgh

than 400 years. The oldest tree in Europe is in Scotland. It has

been alive (3) _____ 3,000 years! Edinburgh has been the capital of Scotland

(4) _____ 1437. Glasgow, the biggest city in Scotland, has the third oldest

underground in the world. It has been in use (5) _____ 1896. Saint Valentine died

on 14th February 269 AD in Glasgow. His grave has been in the city (6) _____ more

than 1,750 years.

► Check

15 How long?

Write present perfect sentences. Add *for* or *since*.

1 *We haven't watched a film since we went to London.*
we / not watch / a film / we went to London

2 _____
I / play / tennis / I was five

3 _____
they / read / books in the library / half an hour

4 _____
we / have / a dog / two months

5 _____
he / have / the same piano teacher / many years

16 Challenge An interview with your English exchange partner

a) You want to interview your English exchange partner. Look at the notes and write your questions. Use the present perfect where neccessary.

1 *How long have you been at your school?*

2 _____

3 _____

4 _____

5 _____

1 how long / be / at your school?

2 how long / live / in your home?

3 what / favourite sport? / how long / play / it?

4 what / favourite computer game? / how long / like / it?

5 who's / best friend? / how long / be / friends?

b) Write your own answers for the questions in a. Use *for* and *since*.

1 _____

2 _____

3 _____

4 _____

5 _____

► Check

17 MIXED GRAMMAR **A brave teenager**

Read the story. Then complete it with the words from the box.

big • for • nervous • hard • harder • ~~has been~~ • has climbed • has talked • since • slowly

Poorna Malavath

Poorna Malavath (1) *has been* _____ famous

(2) _____ she was 13, when she climbed Mount

Everest. She's the youngest girl to climb Everest! Malavath learned to

climb in less than one year! How did she do it? She joined a project

for poor children in Hyderabad, India. The project helps children to do

cool things they would never normally be able to do.

Poorna Malavath

Malavath chose climbing. She loved the mountains and she trained very (3) _____.

She trained (4) _____ than the other

climbers, and the project chose Malavath to climb

Mount Everest. She was very happy: this was her

dream! When Malavath's team arrived at the bottom

of Mount Everest, the mountain looked so

(5) _____.

The team felt (6) _____. They

climbed (7) _____ and carefully, and

eight weeks later, they were at 8,849 m – on top of

Mount Everest. Since then, Malavath

(8) _____ the 'seven summits' – the

seven tallest mountains in the world. And (9) _____ the past ten years, she

(10) _____ to hundreds of poor children. Malavath helps them to live their dreams.

► Check

life

Possessivbegleiter und Possessivpronomen *(Possessive determiners and possessive pronouns)*

Possessivbegleiter und Possessivpronomen zeigen dir an, wem etwas gehört:
• Possessivbegleiter stehen vor einem Nomen.
• Possessivpronomen werden ohne Nomen verwendet.

mit Nomen (Possessivbegleiter)	ohne Nomen (Possessivpronomen)	
my house	*mine*	*This is their car. It's theirs.*
your house	*yours*	*(Das ist ihr Auto. Es ist ihres. / Es gehört ihnen.)*
his / her / its house	*his / hers / its*	*I think it's his pullover. It's his.*
our house	*ours*	*(Ich glaube, es ist sein Pullover. Es ist seiner.)*
your house	*yours*	*I've found this pen. Is it yours?*
their house	*theirs*	*(Ich habe diesen Stift gefunden. Ist es deiner?)*

▶ SB p. 116, p. 193

---

1 Matching

Match the sentences.

1 Is this our video? <u>B</u>

2 That isn't her phone. ___

3 You can use my pen. ___

4 I love their video. ___

5 Can I borrow your camera? ___

6 His video has music on it. ___

A Yours is better than this one.

B Oh yes, it's ours.

C But Adam didn't record the music. It isn't his.

D Theirs was the funniest.

E Mine is the blue one.

F No, it isn't hers.

---

2 Anglesey is my favourite place

(Circle) the correct words.

I'm making a video about the Isle of Anglesey. My / Mine grandparents lived there, and we spent some of our / ours nicest summers on their / theirs farm. It was a very old house – their / theirs was the oldest house in the village. Our / Ours grandfather often told us the greatest ghost stories. My grandmother made Welsh cakes. Her / Hers were the best! Anglesey is still my favourite place. What's your / yours?

Welsh cakes

▶ Check ⮌

3 Exchange partners

Dylan and Owen are writing to their exchange partners.
Complete their chat with possessive pronouns or possessive determiners.

it's = it is / it has
its = sein, ihr

Hi Dylan! Have you written the email to (1) y_____ exchange partner yet? ✓

Oh, hi Owen! Yes, I've written (2) m_____. What about (3) y_____? ✓

I've just sent it. I've told him about (4) m_____ family. ✓

Have you told him about (5) y_____ dog and that it's hurt (6) i_____ leg? ✓

Yes, I've told him the dog barks a lot at the moment. I've told him about (7) o_____ house too. He lives in a flat, and he shares a bedroom with (8) h_____ brother. He won't need to share a room at (9) o_____. ✓

And have you said anything about school? I know that (10) t_____ is very different. ✓

Oh yes, (11) t_____ school has 3,000 students. (12) O_____ is much smaller. ✓

4 What's missing?

Write sentences with the missing pronouns and determiners in the right place.

1 Is this your sister's bag? – I'm not sure, but I think it's.   `hers`

_____

2 The dog is barking because it has lost toy.   `its`

_____

3 I have a cap like that, but is nicer.   `yours`

_____

4 Ryan has a bike like that. In fact, I'm sure it's.   `his`

_____

5 Tom and Simon live in a big flat – is bigger than.   `theirs, mine`

_____

▶ Check ⬎

REVISION: Die Zukunft mit *going to (The going to-future)*

Möchtest du sagen, dass du etwas vorhast oder planst, verwendest du *going to. Going to* hat nichts mit dem deutschen „gehen" zu tun, sondern bedeutet „werden" oder „vorhaben".

A **Bejahte Aussagen** *(Positive statements)*

I'm		
You're		
He's / She's / It's	+ going to	+ verb
We're		
You're		
They're		

Ben is going to visit Ali on Sunday.
(Ben hat vor, am Sonntag Ali zu besuchen.)
They're going to come to the party.
(Sie planen, zur Party zu kommen.)

B **Verneinte Aussagen** *(Negative statements)*

I'm not		
You aren't		
He / She / It isn't	+ going to	+ verb
We aren't		
You aren't		
They aren't		

Ben isn't going to visit Ali on Sunday.
(Ben hat nicht vor, am Sonntag Ali zu besuchen.)
They aren't going to come to the party.
(Sie planen nicht, zur Party zu kommen.)

► SB p. 121, p. 144, p. 194

5 REVISION What are their plans?

a) Complete the sentences. First use the positive form of the going to-future, then use the negative form.

1 go: We **'re going to go** on holiday to Wales. We **aren't going to go** to Spain.

2 play: They _____ rugby. They _____ football.

3 visit: I _____ Cardiff. I _____ Anglesey.

4 sing: She _____ in Welsh. She _____ in English.

5 do: He _____ gymnastics. He _____ judo.

b) Complete the sentences with the phrases from the box.

going • is • isn't • ~~'m~~ • meet • not • not going • 're • 's • you

1 I **'m** going to go swimming today. I'm _____ to wait until tomorrow!

2 We aren't going to _____ after school. Peter _____ going to be busy today.

3 He _____ going to play rugby. He hates it!

4 They _____ going to make some food now because they're hungry.

5 You're _____ going to see your dad today. _____'re going to stay with grandma this afternoon.

6 She _____ going to get the bus. She isn't _____ to walk.

► Check

Erklär-
film

REVISION: Die Zukunft mit *going to*: Fragen und Antworten *(Questions and answers)*

In Fragen vertauschst du das Subjekt und am / is / are:

you are going to → *are you going to?*

Is she going to wait? – Yes, she is.

Are you going to dance? – No, I'm not.

Where are we going to live? – In London.

► SB p. 121, p. 144, p. 194

6 REVISION Tech talk

Write questions. Put the words in the right order.

1 *Are you going to charge your phone now?*
charge / to / are / you / your phone now? / going

2 _____
let / you get this app? / your dad / is / going / to

3 _____
to my Wi-Fi? / are / to / they / connect / going

4 _____
going / are / to / on this link? / we / click

5 _____
to / Simon / is / going / save / the video?

6 _____
going / are / to / you / add / captions?

7 REVISION Digital detox

Gwen and Livia are talking about Livia's digital detox plans. Complete their conversation.

Gwen _____ (you, come) over to my place to play some video games?

Livia No, I_____. Sorry. Mum and I are going to do some digital detox.

Gwen Oh! What _____ (you, do)? Or what aren't you going to do?

Livia Well, I'm not going to use my phone or my computer.

Gwen _____ (your mum, use) her phone or computer?

Livia No, she_____. Only if she needs to do something for her work.

Gwen And _____ (your dad, join) you too?

Livia Yes, he_____. Well, he wants to try at least.

► Check 🔽

8 REVISION **What are their plans for the afternoon?**

a) Write questions.

1 *Is Dylan going to play basketball?*   *No, he isn't.*
(Dylan / play basketball)

2 _____   _____
(Gwen / play basketball)

3 _____   _____
(Flynn / listen to music)

4 _____   _____
(Dylan and Owen / make a cake)

5 _____   _____
(Gwen and Flynn / make a cake)

6 _____   _____
(Gwen / listen to music)

b) Follow the lines to find out what the students are or aren't going to do. Write the answers to the questions in a.

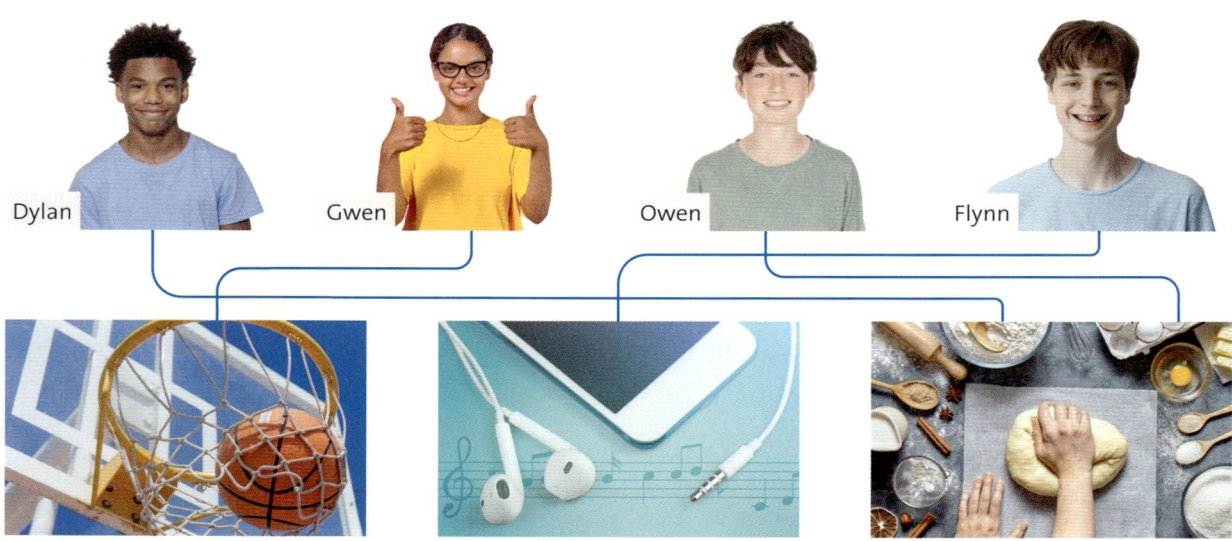

Dylan   Gwen   Owen   Flynn

9 REVISION **What are you going to do this evening?**

a) Write three more questions in the going to-future.

b) What are your plans for this evening? Answer the questions for you?

_____

_____

► Check

Möchtest du sagen, dass etwas wahrscheinlich passieren wird, weil es zum Beispiel bereits Anzeichen dafür gibt, verwendest du *going to*.

Your new teacher is very nice. You're going to like him.
(Dein neuer Lehrer ist sehr nett. Du wirst ihn mögen.)

Look at the dark clouds. It isn't going to be sunny today.
(Sieh die die dunklen Wolken an. Heute wird es nicht sonnig werden.)

► SB p. 145, p. 194

10 Challenge What's going to happen?

Read about the situations and write predictions with *going to*.

1 The score is 3-1 for Manchester United and there's only one minute left in the game.

win: Manchester United *are going to win* _____ the game.

2 Chris and Oliver have just arrived at a great summer camp with lots of amazing activities to do.

enjoy: Chris and Oliver _____ summer camp.

3 Sarah is running for the bus, but she can't see the bus yet.

miss: Sarah _____ the bus.

4 It's the end of the lesson and Dario is still working on the first question of his history test.

finish: Dario _____ his test.

11 Challenge Predictions

Look at the family in the picture and write predictions for their future. You can use the ideas in the box or your own ideas. Write as many predictions as you can.

The family / They The children/parents The boy/girl/dog	enjoy have live play work	football with the dog their own room(s) in the garden happily

The family is going to move into the blue house. _____

_____

_____

_____

_____

_____

► Check 🔖

Relativsätze (Relative clauses)

Möchtest du Personen oder Dinge beschreiben und zusätzliche Informationen über sie geben, verwendest du Relativsätze. Relativsätze werden durch Relativpronomen eingeleitet.

- Für Personen verwendest du das Relativpronomen who.
- Für Dinge verwendest du das Relativpronomen which.
- Mit dem Relativpronomen that kannst du Personen oder Dinge beschreiben.

This is the girl who / that found my dog.
(Das ist das Mädchen, das meinen Hund gefunden hat.)
I know a street which / that has the best shops.
(Ich kenne eine Straße, die die besten Läden hat.)

► SB p. 126, p. 195

12 'Cymru' means 'Wales' in Welsh

a) Circle the right words.

'Cymry' is the adjective for people which / who are Welsh.

The daffodil is a flower which / who is the national symbol of Wales.

Rugby is the sport who / which most Welsh people love.

Charlotte Church is a popular singer who / which is Welsh.

Gareth Bale is a Welsh footballer which / who played for Real Madrid.

Coal mining is something which / who Wales was famous for in the past.

b) **Match the sentence halves.**

1　Cardiff is Wales's biggest city _C_

2　Cardiffians are people ___

3　'Hen Wlad Fy Nhadau' is the national song ___

4　Evan James is the person ___

5　Snowdonia is a national park ___

6　There are over 3.5 million people ___

A　who visit Snowdonia every year.

B　who wrote 'Hen Wlad Fy Nhadau' in 1856.

C　that is also the capital.

D　that all Welsh people know.

E　who come from Cardiff.

F　that gets its name from Wales's highest mountain: Mount Snowdon.

► Check

13 Rugby

a) Read about Rugby in Wales and complete the text with *which* or *who*.

Rugby is a sport (1) _which_ is very popular in Wales. You play rugby

on a pitch (2) _____ is a bit bigger than a football

pitch. There are 15 players on each team. There's a referee

(3) _____ makes sure the players play by the rules. Players

use a ball (4) _____ is similar to football, but it's in the form of an egg.

To score, players need to carry the ball over the 'try line'

(5) _____ is at the other end of the pitch. Players

run with the ball towards the other team's try line. The other

team tries to stop the player (6) _____ is carrying the ball. Players throw the ball

to other players (7) _____ are on their team. There's a goalpost on the try line

(8) _____ is in the form of a big 'H'. Players can

get points when they kick the ball through the top of the 'H'

shape. The rules of rugby aren't easy to learn. There are many

fans (9) _____ can't remember all of the rules!

rugby ball

rugby pitch

b) Find and correct three mistakes in these sentences. Put a tick (✓) if the sentence is correct.

1 Modern rugby comes from a game ~~who~~ schoolboys played at Rugby School in England in

   the 1820s. _which/that_

2 There are at least 50 countries which have international rugby teams. _____

3 The first international rugby match who took place was Scotland against England in 1871.

   _____

4 JPR Williams was a famous Welsh rugby player which died in 2024. _____

5 There are over 100 clubs in Germany who play rugby. _____

6 The best German teams play in the Rugby-Bundesliga which has 16 clubs. _____

► Check 🔽

14 Green energy

Wales uses green energy today. Complete the sentences with the phrases from the box.

that make climate change worse • that uses wind energy to make electricity • which produced coal • which produce green energy • who worked as a minor

1 In the past, Wales had a lot of mines _____.

2 Many years ago, most Welsh people knew somebody _____.

3 When you burn coal, it produces fumes _____.

4 A wind turbine is a machine _____.

5 These are the kind of wind turbines _____.

15 Quiz time!

Complete the quiz questions with *which* or *who*. Then try to answer the quiz questions.

◀ ▶ ⟳ ⌂   www.quiztime.example.com

Quiz time!

1 What's the name of the band [　　　] sang *Don't Look Back In Anger*?

[　　　　　]

2 What's the name of the man [　　　] wrote the lyrics of *Auld Lang Syne*?

[　　　　　]

3 What's the name of the monster [　　　] lives in Loch Ness? [　　　　　]

4 What's the name of a special instrument [　　　] they play in Scotland?

[　　　　　]

5 What's the title of the person [　　　] is the father of Prince William?

[　　　　　]

6 What's the animal [　　　] you can ride on Llandudno Beach?

[　　　　　]

► Check ⬎

Erklär-
film

Challenge: Relativsätze ohne Relativpronomen *(Contact clauses)*

Das Relativpronomen kann als Subjekt oder Objekt des Relativsatzes stehen:

Subjekt	**Objekt**
the man who asked → he asked	*the man (who) I asked → I asked him*
(der Mann, der fragte)	*(der Mann, den ich fragte)*
Steht das Relativpronomen direkt vor dem Verb, dann ist es Subjekt. In diesem Fall darfst du es nicht weglassen.	Ist das Relativpronomen nicht Subjekt, sondern Objekt, kannst du es im Englischen weglassen. Relativsätze ohne Relativpronomen heißen *contact clauses*.
Is this the artist who won the first prize?	*The film I watched yesterday was great.*
I know a shop which sells great ice cream.	*The shoes she's wearing are brand new.*
The bird that sings at night sounds nice.	*This is the girl we met yesterday.*

►SB p. 147, p. 195

---

16 Challenge Cyber bullying

a) Read about cyber bullying. Is the relative pronoun in each sentence the subject or the object of the relative clause? Tick (✓) the right column.

		subject	object
1	Cyber bullying is something that 20% of teenagers have experienced.	☐	☐
2	Cyber bullying is something that we can stop if we try.	☐	☐
3	There are quite a few students who experience cyber bullying at my school.	☐	☐
4	Cyber bullying often comes from people who you know.	☐	☐
5	Some of the messages that they got were not kind.	☐	☐
6	In most countries, there are charities which help young people talk about bullying.	☐	☐

b) In which sentences in a can you leave out the relative pronoun? Write the sentence numbers.

Sentences: _____

c) Read more about bullying. Complete the sentences with *which* or *who* if necessary.
Put a cross (✗) if you don't need a relative pronoun.

1 Bullying is something __X_____ people have always dealt with.

2 In the days before the internet, a bully was someone _____ upset you when you were

   away from your home.

3 But cyber bullying is something _____ can be a problem inside and outside your

   home.

4 There are many people _____ don't tell anyone if they have experienced bullying.

5 It's very important to tell someone _____ you trust about bullying.

►Check

17 `Challenge` Digital life

a) Write sentence. Leave out the relative pronoun if you don't need one.

1 that you use / to show how you're feeling / an emoji is a small picture

An emoji is a small picture you use to show how you're feeling.

2 which can tell you / a smart watch is a device / more than just the time

_____

3 video stories online / a vlogger is a person / who posts

_____

4 an influencer is a person / who you follow / on social media

_____

5 a 'bio' is information / about a person's life / that tells you

_____

6 which you use to make / a photograph look different / a filter is something

_____

b) Match the sentence halves. Add *that* if necessary.

1 A follower is someone C *that* | A allows you to share things online.

2 Social media is something ___ _____ | B you create for your social media.

3 Make-up is something ___ _____ | C follows you on social media.

4 Editing software is something ___ _____ | D you wear on your face to make it look better.

5 Content is something ___ _____ | E you use to do jobs on a device.

6 An app is a tool ___ _____ | F you use to change the content of photos.

► Check

18 MIXED GRAMMAR Colour by numbers

Colour in the picture.

- Possessive pronouns = yellow
- Possessive determiners = green
- Relative pronouns to talk about things = red
- Relative pronouns to talk about people = orange

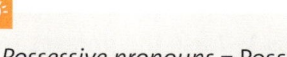

Possessive pronouns = Possessivpronomen
Possessive determiners = Possessivbegleiter

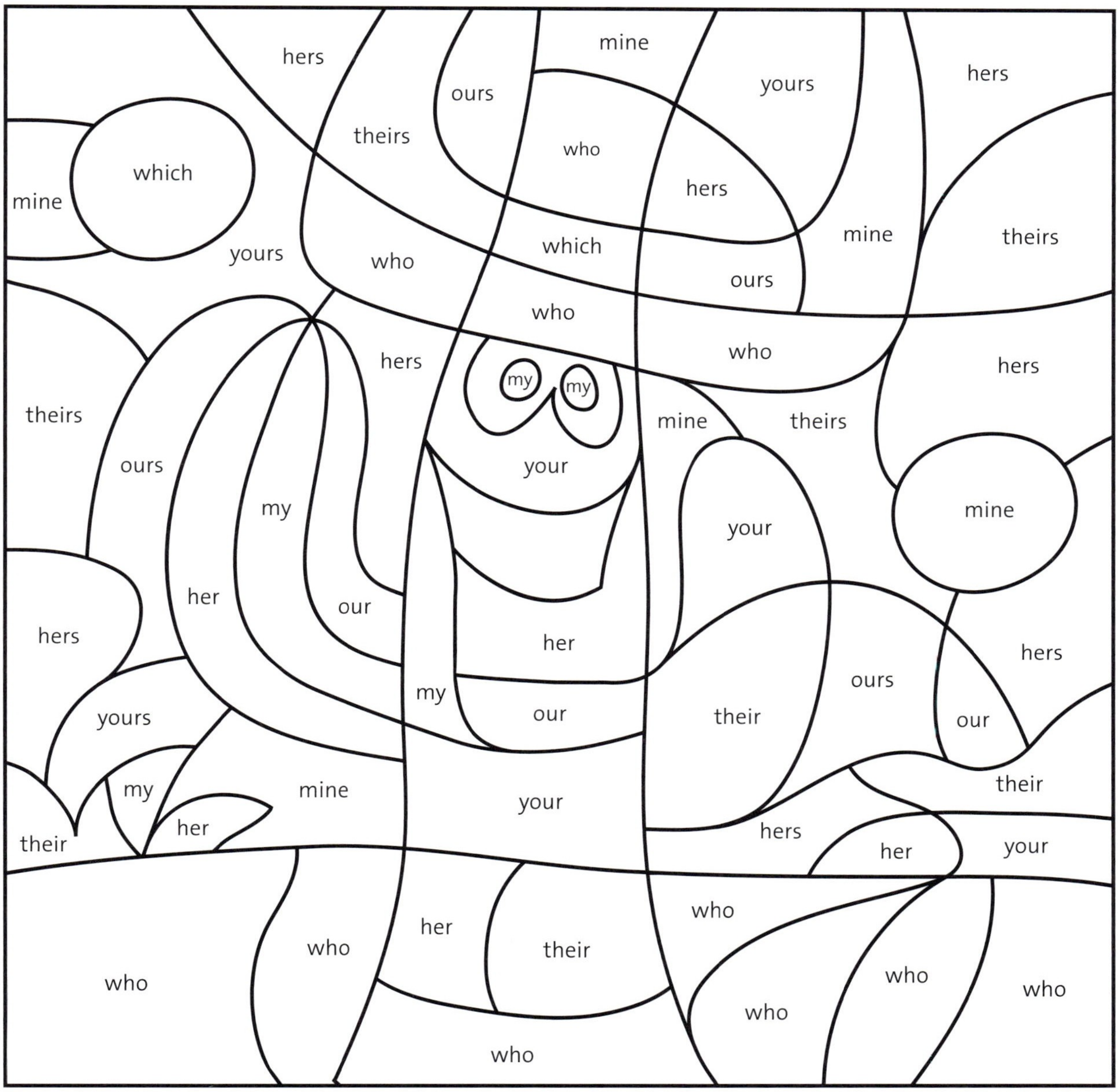

hers
mine
ours
yours
hers
theirs
who
which
mine
mine
hers
which
theirs
yours
who
ours
who
theirs
who
hers
who
hers
my my
theirs
mine
mine
your
your
my
mine
her
our
her
ours
hers
her
mine
ours
your
their
our
my
mine
your
their
hers
theirs
her
your
their
who
who
her
their
who
who
who
who
who
who

▶ Check

19 MIXED GRAMMAR Dylan and Owen's next video

a) Dylan and Owen are making a new video for their social media.
Complete their conversation:

- For gaps 1–7 use the phrases from box 1.
- For gaps A–H use the words from box 2.

1
Are we going to add • are going to check •
~~Are we going to upload~~ • 'm going to cut •
is going to be • This is going to be • Yes, we are.

2
hers • mine • our • ours •
which (2x) • who (2x)

Dylan (1) *Are we going to upload* the new video tonight?

Owen (2) _____ I have all of the video

clips. Some of them are your clips and some of them

are (A) _____. I think we have

about twelve minutes of video in total.

Dylan And we want the final video to be about 30 seconds, right?

Owen Yes, 25–30 seconds is good. I (3) _____ the parts

(B) _____ we don't need. Then you and Alice

(4) _____ the edited video.

Dylan Alice? Is she the girl (C) _____ made the video about Swansea?

Owen Yes, she is. I think this video (5) _____

(D) _____ most popular one. So we want something

(E) _____ is …

Dylan … perfect!

Owen Perfect! Exactly. That's why there are three of us (F) _____ are going to

check it.

Dylan (6) _____ captions on this video?

Owen No, I don't think so. Alice didn't have captions on (G) _____, so I don't

think we need them on (H) _____.

Dylan OK! (7) _____ fun!   ▶ Check ⬇

REVISION: Verneinte Sätze (*Negative sentences*)

Möchtest du sagen, dass etwas nicht passiert, passierte oder passieren wird, brauchst du ein Hilfsverb, das du verneinst.

do	Juan *doesn't* play the violin. (*simple present*) Paula *didn't* take part in the dance competition last week. (*simple past*)
be	I'm *not* singing at the moment because I'm talking. (*present progressive*) I'm *not* going to join the school band next year. (*going to-future*)
have	Filiz *hasn't* been to Ireland. (*present perfect*)
will	My parents *won't* buy me a computer for my birthday. (*will-future*)

---

1 REVISION **South Voice: Orla**

Write negative sentences.

1 I know a lot about the Troubles.

   I don't know a lot about the Troubles.

2 My dad went to Northern Ireland last year.

   _____

3 I'm going to look at the Peace Walls.

   _____

4 We've lived in Dublin since 2021.

   _____

5 I'll be in Northern Ireland for a month.

   _____

6 My mum wants to go to the Titanic Belfast museum.

   _____

7 I'm looking forward to the long journey.

   _____

► Check

2 REVISION North Voice: Jack

a) Jack is doing an interview. Read Jack's answers. Then write the questions.

1 <u>Where do you go to school?</u>
   do / where / to school? / you / go

> I go to a protestant school.

2 _____
   your school? / you / do / like

> Yes, I do.

3 _____
   you / do / what / will / after school?

> I'll work in my parents' B&B.

4 _____
   did / you / why / the North and South Voices project? / like

> I think it was a great project.

5 _____
   next? / to do / going / you / are / what

> I'm going to take part in other great projects.

b) There are more interview questions. Complete them with the words in the box.
   Tipp: Look at the answers to find the right words.

> are • did • do (2×) • has • will

1 Where _____ you live? – I live in Belfast in Northern Ireland.

2 Where _____ you live when you're older? – I'll stay here!

3 _____ you go to the Giant's Causeway last week? – Yes, I did. It was a day trip.

4 Why _____ you like the Giant's Causeway? – Because you can climb on cool rocks.

5 What _____ you studying at school right now? – We're learning about the Troubles.

6 _____ that period of history been interesting? – Yes, it has. It's been interesting, but very sad.

► Check

Im Englischen ist die Wortstellung immer subject – verb – object. Das gilt sowohl für Hauptsätze als auch für Nebensätze.

Hauptsatz (*main sentence*)				Nebensatz (*subordinate sentence*)		
subject	verb	object		subject	verb	object
I	*can't buy*	*the tickets*	*because*	*I*	*can't find*	*my money.*
Ms Evans	*listened to*	*an audio guide*	*while*	*she*	*walked*	*through Dublin.*
Zane	*will make*	*dinner*	*after*	*he*	*cleaned*	*his room.*

Wörter, die Nebensätze einleiten sind z. B. Konjunktionen (*after, because, if, so, when*) oder Relativpronomen (*that, which, who*).

3 REVISION **Our trip to Dublin**

a) Read about Nila's trip to Dublin and complete her sentences with the phrases from the box.

> after we had • because we don't have • so we booked •
> so we had • when we arrived • while the taxi took

1 We wanted to stay in a B&B, _____ one online.

Dublin

2 We took the train to Dublin _____ a car.

3 We played card games, _____ something

to do on the train.

4 We got into a taxi _____ at Dublin train station.

5 I looked out of the car window _____ us to the B&B.

6 We went to our room at the B&B _____ a delicious dinner.

b) The word order is wrong in some of Nila's sentences. Find four mistakes and write the correct word order.

1 The next morning, we went downstairs after showers we had. _____

2 We looked at a map because we planned a long walk. _____

3 We talked about the route while we our breakfast ate. _____

4 Then we filled our water bottles, so had we water for the walk. _____

5 But it started to rain when we the B&B left! _____

6 We went back into the B&B while we waited for the rain to stop. _____

► Check

Challenge: Simple present oder present progressive (*Simple present or present progressive*)

Möchtest du sagen, dass etwas regelmäßig stattfindet oder immer so ist, verwendest du das simple present. Signalwörter sind die Häufigkeitsadverbien (*always, often, sometimes, never, …*) oder *every day, every week, …*

I often go to bed before 9 o'clock.
Timo doesn't like maths lessons.
Do you speak German at home? – Yes, I do. / No, I don't.

Wenn du sagen möchtest, dass etwas genau in diesem Moment stattfindet oder wenn du Bilder beschreibst, verwendest du das present progressive. Du verwendest es oft mit Zeitangaben wie *now, at the moment, today.*

Luca is making breakfast for his parents at the moment.
Carmen isn't smiling in the photo.
Are Cem and Liz visiting their grandparents today? – Yes, they are. / No, they aren't.

► SB pp. 182–184

4 Challenge Breakfast at the B&B

a) Orla and her mum are in Belfast. Read the sentences and (circle) the signal words. Then highlight the verbs. Is the sentence simple present or present progressive?

	simple present	present progressive
1 Jack serves the breakfasts every day during the holidays.	☐	☐
2 Jack is serving Orla and her mum today.	☐	☐
3 He's taking their breakfast order right now.	☐	☐
4 Orla never eats meat.	☐	☐
5 Orla usually orders a vegetarian breakfast.	☐	☐
6 Orla's mum is having a full cooked breakfast at the moment.	☐	☐

b) Read about Orla and her mum and complete the sentences with the simple present or present progressive form of the verbs in brackets. Look at the signal words for help.

Right now, Orla and her mum (1) _____ (talk) about their plans for the day.

Orla always (2) _____ (want) to go to markets. Orla's mum usually

(3) _____ (prefer) something historical. They (4) _____

(ask) Jack now. Jack often (5) _____ (recommend) the black cab tour of Belfast.

The tour guides usually (6) _____ (know) many interesting facts. Jack

(7) _____ (give) Orla and her mum information about the black cab tour now.

Orla (8) _____ (go) to markets every week, so today she'll join her mum on a

black cab tour at 10.30.

► Check 🔖

Erklär-
film

Challenge: Present perfect oder simple past (*Present perfect or simple past*)

Mit dem present perfect sagst du, dass etwas in der Vergangenheit geschehen ist. Der genaue Zeitpunkt ist unwichtig oder unbekannt. Signalwörter für das *present perfect* sind unbestimmte Zeitangaben, z. B. *not … yet, ever, for/since, lots of times.*

Sarah has visited her aunt and uncle lots of times.
We haven't talked to our parents yet.
Have you ever been to Belfast? — Yes, I have. / No, I haven't.

Mit dem simple past sagst du, wann etwas in der Vergangenheit geschehen ist, oft mit genauen Zeitangaben wie *yesterday, last summer, two days ago, in 2023.*

Leo travelled to Dublin last summer.
I didn't have lunch yesterday.
What did you do last weekend?

► SB pp. 185–186, pp. 192–193

5   Challenge   Irish holiday experiences

a) Read about holidays in Ireland. **Highlight** the signal word in each sentence.

b) For sentences 1–5 (circle) the correct words. For sentences 6–10 complete the sentence with the present perfect or simple past form of the verbs in brackets.

1 Jannis hasn't visited / didn't visit Belfast since 2023.

2 Have you ever visited / Did you ever visit Northern Ireland?

3 Maja has flown / flew to Dublin last month.

4 Has Jack walked / Did Jack walk on Giant's Causeway last week?

5 Nick and Sarah haven't enjoyed / didn't enjoy the Murals tour at the weekend.

6 Alex _____ (try) the food on St. George's

Market two days ago.

7 I _____ never _____

(watch) a match at Windsor Park stadium in Belfast.

8 Yusuf _____ (love) his class trip to the

Titanic Belfast museum yesterday.

9 Ethan _____ (not send) any postcards yet.

10 _____ Ella _____ (be) to Cork lots of times?

► Check

Belfast

Giant's Causeway

Titanic Belfast

Unit 1 London: City life

▶ Grammarmaster p. 4

Erklär-film

REVISION: Die Zukunft mit *will (The will-future)*

Das *will-future* verwendest du für Dinge, die vermutlich in der Zukunft geschehen werden, oder für spontane Entschlüsse und Hilfsangebote. Du bildest es mit *will* und dem Infinitiv des Verbs.

A **Bejahte Aussagesätze** *(Positive statements)*			B **Verneinte Aussagesätze** *(Negative statements)*		
We	will / 'll	go hiking.	We	will not / won't	go hiking.
It	will / 'll	be sunny tomorrow.	It	will not / won't	be sunny tomorrow.

▶ SB p. 17, p. 43, p. 186

▶ Grammarmaster p. 5

Erklär-film

REVISION: Die Zukunft mit *will*: Fragen und Kurzantworten *(Questions and short answers)*

Bei Fragen stellst du *will* an den Satzanfang. Hat die Frage ein Fragewort, steht dieses noch vor *will*.

Will they go shopping? – Yes, they will. / No, they won't.

Will she visit her grandmother? – Yes, she will. / No, she won't.

Who will you invite to your party?

When will we arrive in London?

▶ SB p. 17, p. 43, p. 186

▶ Grammarmaster pp. 6–8

Erklär-film

Bedingungssätze Typ I *(Conditional sentences type I)*

Mit Bedingungssätzen sagst du, was unter bestimmten Bedingungen geschehen wird: *Falls … dann.*

Bedingungssätze bestehen aus zwei Teilen:
- einem Nebensatz mit *if (if-clause)* im *simple present*, der die Bedingung nennt,
- einem Hauptsatz *(main clause)* mit *will*, *'ll* oder *won't*, der die Folge nennt.

Der Nebensatz *(if-clause)* kann auch <u>nach</u> dem Hauptsatz *(main clause)* stehen. Dann setzt du kein Komma.

Bedingung *(if-clause)* → Folge *(main clause)*	Folge *(main clause)* ← Bedingung *(if-clause)*
If you need help, I'll be there.	*I'll be there if you need help.*
(Falls du Hilfe brauchst, bin ich da.)	*(Ich bin da, falls du Hilfe brauchst.)*
If the bus is too late, we'll miss the train.	*We'll miss the train if the bus is too late.*
(Falls der Bus zu spät ist, verpassen wir den Zug.)	*(Wir verpassen den Zug, falls der Bus zu spät ist.)*

▶ SB p. 21, p. 187

▶ Grammarmaster pp. 9–10

Erklär-film

REVISION: Das simple past *(The simple past)*

Mit dem *simple past* sagst du, was in der Vergangenheit geschehen ist.

A Bejahte Aussagen *(Positive statements)*

Bei regelmäßigen Verben hängst du *-ed* an den Infinitiv des Verbs an: *jump – jumped, walk – walked*
Unregelmäßige Verben musst du auswendig lernen: *do – did, go – went, have – had*

B Verneinte Aussagen *(Negative statements)*

Möchtest du sagen, dass etwas nicht geschah, setzt du *didn't* vor den Infinitiv des Verbs: *didn't jump, didn't go*

C Fragen *(Questions)*

Bei Fragen stellst du *Did* an den Anfang der Frage. Ein Fragewort kommt noch davor.

Did you talk to Lisa yesterday?

Where did you go on holiday last summer?

▶ SB p. 27, p. 46, pp. 185–186, pp. 294–295

Unit 2 Manchester: Who we are

▶ Grammarmaster p. 12

Erklär-film

REVISION: Die Steigerung der Adjektive mit *-er / -est* (*The comparison of adjectives with -er/-est*)

Adjektive kannst du steigern und in Vergleichen benutzen. Bei einsilbigen Adjektiven und bei zweisilbigen Adjektiven, die auf *-y* enden, hängst du *-er / -est* an das Adjektiv:

- *small → smaller (Komparativ = erste Steigerungsform)*
- *tall → the tallest (Superlativ = Höchstform)*

> *The cat is smaller than the dog.*
> *(Die Katze ist kleiner als der Hund.)*
> *Ethan is the tallest student at school.*
> *(Ethan ist der größte Schüler der Schule.)*

▶ SB p. 50, p. 75, p. 187

▶ Grammarmaster p. 13

Erklär-film

REVISION: Die Steigerung der Adjektive mit *more / most* (*The comparison of adjectives with more/most*)

Bei längeren (vor allem dreisilbigen) Adjektiven setzt du more / most vor das Adjektiv:

- *interesting → more interesting*
  (Komparativ = erste Steigerungsform)
- *expensive → most expensive*
  (Superlativ = Höchstform)

> *The book is more interesting than the movie.*
> *(Das Buch ist interessanter als der Film.)*
> *The most expensive cities are Hongkong and Zurich.*
> *(Die teuersten Städte sind Hongkong und Zürich.)*

▶ SB p. 50, p. 75, p. 188

▶ Grammarmaster p. 14

Paarwörter (*Pair nouns*)

Paarwörter bezeichnen Dinge, die aus zwei gleichen Teilen bestehen, z.B. Kleidungsstücke, Werkzeuge oder Brillen. Diese Wörter stehen immer im Plural. Die zugehörigen Verben, Begleiter oder Pronomen stehen ebenfalls im Plural.
These jeans are very tight. (Diese Jeans ist sehr eng.)
Have you seen my glasses? I can't find them. (Hast du meine Brille gesehen? Ich kann sie nicht finden.)
Your headphones don't look cheap. (Deine Kopfhörer sehen nicht günstig aus.)

Paarwörter können einen oder mehrere Gegenstände bezeichnen. Möchtest du die genaue Anzahl angeben, stellst du *a pair of* voran.
I bought a pair of scissors yesterday. (Ich habe gestern eine Schere gekauft.)
Hannah put two pairs of leggings into her bag. (Hannah legte zwei Leggings in ihre Tasche.)

▶ SB p. 52

▶ Grammarmaster p. 15

Erklär-film

Modale Hilfsverben: Erlaubnis und Verbot (*Modal verbs: permission and prohibition*)

Die meisten modalen Hilfsverben haben nur eine Form. Sie stehen im Infinitiv (in der Grundform).
- **Erlaubnis:** *I can / am allowed to play outside with the dog? (Ich darf draußen mit dem Hund spielen?)*
- **Verbot:** *Dad says I can't / mustn't / am not allowed to go to the zoo today. (Papa sagt, ich darf heute nicht in den Zoo gehen.)*
- **Höfliche Bitte:** *May / Could I have some sugar, please? (Darf ich bitte etwas Zucker haben?)*

Challenge Möchtest du über die Vergangenheit oder Zukunft sprechen, verwendest du *be (not) allowed to.*
I was allowed to stay at Ava's house after the party. (Ich durfte nach der Party bei Ava bleiben.)
I won't be allowed to go camping next summer. (Ich werde nächsten Sommer nicht zelten dürfen.)

▶ SB p. 55, p. 77, p. 188

▶ Grammarmaster p. 16

Erklär-
film

Modale Hilfsverben: Notwendigkeit, Zwang *(Modal verbs: necessity, compulsion)*

Mit *must* oder *have to / has to* sagst du, was jemand tun muss. Mit *don't have to / doesn't have to* oder *needn't* sagst du, was jemand nicht zu tun braucht.
Lukasz must / has to be home by 8.30 p.m. *(Lukasz muss 20:30 Uhr zu Hause sein.)*
We needn't / don't have to hurry. *(Wir brauchen uns nicht zu beeilen.)*

Challenge *Must* hat nur eine Form. Möchtest du etwas über die Vergangenheit oder Zukunft sagen verwendest du *have to / has to*.
I had to tidy my room yesterday. *(Ich musste gestern mein Zimmer aufräumen.)*
Moni will have to invite us all to her party. *(Moni wird uns alle zu ihrer Party einladen müssen.)*

▶ SB p. 55, p. 77, p. 189

▶ Grammarmaster p. 17

Erklär-
film

Modale Hilfsverben: Fähigkeit *(Modal verbs: ability)*

Möchtest du sagen, dass jemand etwas tun oder nicht tun kann, verwendest du *can / can't* oder *be (not) able to*.
Penguins can / are able to swim, but they can't / aren't able to fly.
(Pinguine können schwimmen, aber sie können nicht fliegen.)

Challenge *Be (not) able to* hat auch Vergangenheits- und Zukunftsformen.
My mum was able to dance well when she was young. *(Meine Mutter konnte gut tanzen, als sie jung war.)*
You'll be able to speak English soon. *(Du wirst bald Englisch sprechen können.)*

▶ SB p. 77, p. 189

▶ Grammarmaster p. 18

Erklär-
film

Modale Hilfsverben: Möglichkeit und Rat *(Modal verbs: possibility and advice)*

May, might und *could* verwendest du, wenn du sagen möchtest, dass etwas möglich ist.
It may be sunny tomorrow. *(Es könnte morgen sonnig sein. / Vielleicht ist es morgen sonnig.)*
This could be a way out. *(Das könnte ein Ausweg sein.)*
They might get their first child soon. *(Sie werden / könnten vielleicht bald ihr erstes Kind bekommen.)*

Möchtest du jemandem einen Rat geben, verwendest du *should* oder *shouldn't*.
You should take your umbrella — it's rainy outside. *(Du solltest deinen Regenschirm mitnehmen – draußen regnet es.)*
You shouldn't eat so much chocolate and cake. *(Du solltest nicht so viel Schokolade und Kuchen essen.)*

▶ SB pp. 55–56, p. 189

▶ Grammarmaster pp. 19–20

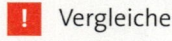 Reflexivpronomen und *each other (Reflexive pronouns and each other)*

A Mit Reflexivpronomen sagst du, dass jemand etwas selbst tut. Sie enden auf *-self/-selves*.
  Für jede Person gibt es eine eigene Form, die du lernen musst.

  I enjoy myself.   *We enjoy ourselves.*
  You enjoy yourself.   *You enjoy yourselves.*
  He enjoys himself.   *They enjoy themselves.*
  She enjoys herself.
  It enjoys itself.

B Möchtest du sagen, dass Menschen etwas gegenseitig tun, verwendest du *each other*.
  We like each other a lot. *(Wir mögen uns (gegenseitig) sehr.)*

! Vergleiche:

Emma and Jana took photos of themselves. | *Emma and Jana took photos of each other.*
(= Emma und Jana haben Fotos gemacht, auf denen sie zusammen zu sehen sind.) | *(= Emma hat Fotos von Jana gemacht, und Jana hat Fotos von Emma gemacht. Sie haben sich gegenseitig fotografiert.)*

▶ SB p. 58, p. 190

Unit 3 Scotland: Adventure

▶ Grammarmaster pp. 22–23

Erklär-
film

REVISION: Adverbien der Art und Weise *(Adverbs of manner)*

Adverbien der Art und Weise beschreiben, wie du etwas tust oder wie etwas geschieht. Sie beziehen sich auf ein Verb. Die meisten Adverbien bildest du durch Anfügen von *-ly* an ein Adjektiv.

Adjektiv	Adverb	
clear	clearly	Mila speaks slowly and clearly.
slow	slowly	*(Mila spricht langsam und deutlich.)*

Manchmal gibt es Unregelmäßigkeiten bei der Schreibung oder Sonderformen:

angry → angrily	good → well	Clara speaks German very well.
happy → happily	fast → fast	Andrew can run very fast.
full → fully	hard → hard	Jonathan worked hard.

▶ SB p. 84, p. 190

▶ Grammarmaster p. 24

Adjektive nach Zustandsverben *(Adjectives after state verbs)*

Nach Verben, die einen Zustand oder eine Eigenschaft beschreiben (wie jemand oder etwas ist), steht ein Adjektiv, kein Adverb. Solche Verben sind *be, become, feel* (sich fühlen), *look* (aussehen), *seem, smell, sound, taste*.

This sounds good.
The doctor was very careful.
I feel so happy today.
The new house looks nice.
The food smells and tastes really horrible.

▶ SB p. 92, p. 191

▶ Grammarmaster pp. 25–26

Challenge: Die Steigerung der Adverbien *(Comparison of adverbs)*

Adverbien kannst du ebenso wie Adjektive steigern und in Vergleichen benutzen. Bei *-ly*-Adverbien bildest du die erste Steigerungsform (Komparativ) mit *more* und die Höchstform (Superlativ) mit *most* vor dem Adverb.

Could you please drive more carefully?
(Könntest du bitte vorsichtiger fahren?)
The old Lady walks more slowly than her dog.
(Die alte Dame geht langsamer als ihr Hund.)
Who dances (the) most beautifully?
(Wer tanzt am schönsten?)

Bei kurzen (meist einsilbigen) Adverbien hängst du *-er* für den Komparativ und *-est* für den Superlativ an das Adverb.

My brother can run faster than me.
(Mein Bruder kann schneller rennen als ich.)
Grandpa speaks the loudest at Christmas dinner.
(Opa spricht beim Weihnachtsessen am lautesten.)

Merke dir diese Ausnahmen:
• well → better → (the) best
• badly → worse → (the) worst

Fatima plays football better than her brother.
(Fatima spielt besser Fußball als ihr Bruder.)

▶ SB p. 111, p. 191

▶ Grammarmaster pp. 27–28

Erklär-
film

REVISION: Das present perfect *(The present perfect)*

Mit dem *present perfect* sagst du, dass jemand etwas gemacht oder nicht gemacht hat. Der genaue Zeitpunkt ist unwichtig oder unbekannt und wird nicht genannt. Signalwörter für das *present perfect* sind: *already, just, ever, never, not yet, once, twice, lots of times*

I have never seen this movie.
(Ich habe diesen Film noch nie gesehen.)
Has Aubrey ever been to Paris?
(Ist Aubrey schon einmal in Paris gewesen?)
Lucas hasn't gone to the museum yet.
(Lucas ist noch nicht ins Museum gegangen.)

▶ SB p. 87, pp. 192–193, pp. 294–295

Erklär-
film

Das present perfect mit *since* oder *for* (*The present perfect with* since *or* for)

► Grammarmaster pp. 45–46

Mit dem *present perfect* sagst du auch, wie lange etwas schon andauert. Du verwendest:

• *since* um zu sagen, wann etwas begonnen hat:
  since 8 o'clock in the morning, *since* July
• *for* um zu sagen, wie lange etwas schon andauert:
  for seven months, *for* six days

They *have lived* in this country *since* 2019.
(Sie leben seit 2019 in diesem Land.)
Mila *has been* in our school *for* eight months.
(Mila ist seit acht Monaten auf unserer Schule.)
Grandma *has visited* us *for* two weeks.
(Oma hat uns zwei Wochen lang besucht.)

► SB p. 89, p. 193

Unit 4 Wales: Digital life

► Grammarmaster pp. 48–49

Possessivbegleiter und Possessivpronomen (*Possessive determiners and possessive pronouns*)

Possessivbegleiter und Possessivpronomen zeigen dir an, wem etwas gehört:
• Possessivbegleiter stehen vor einem Nomen.
• Possessivpronomen werden ohne Nomen verwendet.

mit Nomen (Possessivbegleiter)	ohne Nomen (Possessivpronomen)
my house	*mine*
your house	*yours*
his / her / its house	*his / hers / its*
our house	*ours*
your house	*yours*
their house	*theirs*

This is *their* car. It's *theirs*.
(Das ist ihr Auto. Es ist ihres. / Es gehört ihnen.)
I think it's *his* pullover. It's *his*.
(Ich glaube, es ist sein Pullover. Es ist seiner.)
I've found this pen. Is it *yours*?
(Ich habe diesen Stift gefunden. Ist es deiner?)

► SB p. 116, p. 193

► Grammarmaster pp. 50–52

Erklär-
film

REVISION: Die Zukunft mit *going to* (*The going to-future*)

Möchtest du sagen, dass du etwas vorhast oder planst, verwendest du *going to*. *Going to* hat nichts mit dem deutschen „gehen" zu tun, sondern bedeutet „werden" oder „vorhaben".

A **Bejahte Aussagen** (*Positive statements*)

I'm		
You're		
He's / She's / It's	+ going to	+ verb
We're		
You're		
They're		

Ben is going to visit Ali on Sunday.
(Ben hat vor, am Sonntag Ali zu besuchen.)
They're going to come to the party.
(Sie planen, zur Party zu kommen.)

B **Verneinte Aussagen** (*Negative statements*)

I'm not		
You aren't		
He / She / It isn't	+ going to	+ verb
We aren't		
You aren't		
They aren't		

Ben isn't going to visit Ali on Sunday.
(Ben hat nicht vor, am Sonntag Ali zu besuchen.)
They aren't going to come to the party.
(Sie planen nicht, zur Party zu kommen.)

► SB p. 121, p. 144, p. 194

► Grammarmaster p. 53

Challenge: Vorhersagen mit *going to* *(Predictions with going to)*

Möchtest du sagen, dass etwas wahrscheinlich passieren wird, weil es zum Beispiel bereits Anzeichen dafür gibt, verwendest du *going to*.

Your new teacher is very nice. You're going to like him.
(Dein neuer Lehrer ist sehr nett. Du wirst ihn mögen.)

Look at the dark clouds. It isn't going to be sunny today.
(Sieh die die dunklen Wolken an. Heute wird es nicht sonnig werden.)

► SB p. 145, p. 194

► Grammarmaster pp. 54–56

Erklär-film

Relativsätze *(Relative clauses)*

Möchtest du Personen oder Dinge beschreiben und zusätzliche Informationen über sie geben, verwendest du Relativsätze. Relativsätze werden durch Relativpronomen eingeleitet.

- Für Personen verwendest du das Relativpronomen who.
- Für Dinge verwendest du das Relativpronomen which.
- Mit dem Relativpronomen that kannst du Personen oder Dinge beschreiben.

This is the girl who / that found my dog.
(Das ist das Mädchen, das meinen Hund gefunden hat.)

I know a street which / that has the best shops.
(Ich kenne eine Straße, die die besten Läden hat.)

► SB p. 126, p. 195

► Grammarmaster pp. 57–58

Erklär-film

Challenge: Relativsätze ohne Relativpronomen *(Contact clauses)*

Das Relativpronomen kann als Subjekt oder Objekt des Relativsatzes stehen:

Subjekt	**Objekt**
the man who asked → he asked	*the man (who) I asked → I asked him*
(der Mann, der fragte)	*(der Mann, den ich fragte)*

Steht das Relativpronomen direkt vor dem Verb, dann ist es Subjekt. In diesem Fall darfst du es nicht weglassen.

Is this the artist who won the first prize?

I know a shop which sells great ice cream.

The bird that sings at night sounds nice.

Ist das Relativpronomen nicht Subjekt, sondern Objekt, kannst du es im Englischen weglassen. Relativsätze ohne Relativpronomen heißen *contact clauses*.

The film I watched yesterday was great.

The shoes she's wearing are brand new.

This is the girl we met yesterday.

► SB p. 147, p. 195

Unit 5 Two Irelands: Together

► Grammarmaster p. 61

REVISION: Verneinte Sätze *(Negative sentences)*

Möchtest du sagen, dass etwas nicht passiert, passierte oder passieren wird, brauchst du ein Hilfsverb, das du verneinst.

do	*Juan doesn't play the violin. (simple present)*
	Paula didn't take part in the dance competition last week. (simple past)
be	*I'm not singing at the moment because I'm talking. (present progressive)*
	I'm not going to join the school band next year. (going to-future)
have	*Filiz hasn't been to Ireland. (present perfect)*
will	*My parents won't buy me a computer for my birthday. (will-future)*

► Grammarmaster p. 62

REVISION: Fragen und Antworten (*Questions and answers*)

Bei Fragen im Englischen steht das Hilfsverb am Satzanfang. Ein Fragewort steht noch davor.

do	*Do you like fish and chips? – Yes, I do. / No, I don't.* (simple present)
	Where did you put my books? (simple past)
be	*Why is Camilla crying?* (present progressive)
	Are we going to stay in a B&B next holiday? – Yes, we are. / No, we aren't. (going to-future)
have	*Has Henry invited you to his party yet? – Yes, he has. / No, he hasn't.* (present perfect)
will	*Will robots do our jobs in the future? – Yes, they will. / No, they won't.* (will-future)

► Grammarmaster p. 63

REVISION: Nebensätze (*Subordinate clauses*)

In englischen Haupt- und Nebensätzen ist die Wortstellung immer subject – verb – object.

Hauptsatz (*main sentence*)   Nebensatz (*subordinate sentence*)

subject	verb	object		subject	verb	object
I	*can't buy*	*the tickets*	*because*	*I*	*can't find*	*my money.*
Ms Evans	*listened to*	*an audio guide*	*while*	*she*	*walked*	*through Dublin.*
Zane	*will make*	*dinner*	*after*	*he*	*cleaned*	*his room.*

► Grammarmaster p. 64

Erklär-film

Challenge: Simple present oder present progressive (*Simple present or present progressive*)

Möchtest du sagen, dass etwas regelmäßig stattfindet oder immer so ist, verwendest du das simple present. Signalwörter sind die Häufigkeitsadverbien (*always, often, sometimes, never, …*) oder *every day, every week, …*

I often go to bed before 9 o'clock.
Timo doesn't like maths lessons.
Do you speak German at home? – Yes, I do. / No, I don't.

Wenn du sagen möchtest, dass etwas genau in diesem Moment stattfindet oder wenn du Bilder beschreibst, verwendest du das present progressive. Du verwendest es oft mit Zeitangaben wie *now, at the moment, today.*

Luca is making breakfast for his parents at the moment.
Carmen isn't smiling in the photo.
Are Cem and Liz visiting their grandparents today? – Yes, they are. / No, they aren't.

► SB pp. 182–184

► Grammarmaster p. 65

Erklär-film

Challenge: Present perfect oder simple past (*Present perfect or simple past*)

Mit dem present perfect sagst du, dass etwas in der Vergangenheit geschehen ist. Der genaue Zeitpunkt ist unwichtig oder unbekannt. Signalwörter für das *present perfect* sind unbestimmte Zeitangaben, z. B. *not … yet, ever, for/since, lots of times.*

Sarah has visited her aunt and uncle lots of times.
We haven't talked to our parents yet.
Have you ever been to Belfast? – Yes, I have. / No, I haven't.

Mit dem simple past sagst du, wann etwas in der Vergangenheit geschehen ist, oft mit genauen Zeitangaben wie *yesterday, last summer, two days ago, in 2023.*

Leo travelled to Dublin last summer.
I didn't have lunch yesterday.
What did you do last weekend?

► SB pp. 185–186, pp. 192–193